Adventu

Adventurous moneymaking

from Central Europe to Wall Street

Thomas Fellegi

Stock Trend

Copyright © Thomas Fellegi 2006

The moral rights of the author have been asserted

First published 2006

All rights reserved. No part of this publication may be reproduced, stored in a retrieval system, or transmitted, in any form or by any means, without the prior written permission of the publisher, nor be otherwise circulated in any form of binding or cover other than that in which it is published and without a similar condition being imposed on the subsequent purchaser.

REUTERS

Republication or redissemination of the contents of the charts is expressly prohibited without the prior written consent of Reuters Limited. Copyright © Reuters Limited. All rights reserved.

British Library Cataloguing in Publication data
A catalogue record for this book is available from the British Library

Library of Congress Cataloguing in Publication Data

ISBN-10: 0-9551976-0-0
ISBN-13: 978-0-9551976-0-4

Copyedited by Kathi Hughes

Published by Stock Trend Publishing
23 Harrington Square, London NW1 2JJ, UK
15 West 72nd St, Apt 21S, New York, NY 10023

Printed and bound in Germany by GGP Media GMBH, Pössneck.

CONTENTS

Prologue • 9

PART ONE: THE STORY • 11

1. Moneymaking as a student • 13
    'Private import' • 13
    Escape to hard currencies • 16
    Polish markets and German tourists • 19
    The East German mark • 23
    My first steps on the stock market • 25
    'Shopping tourism' in Austria • 28
    The Czechoslovakian crown • 30

2. The compensation note • 33
    The idea • 33
    The Mafia • 36
    Note speculation • 38
    Back to the stock market • 41
    The OTC market • 43

3. The way to sophisticated markets • 47
    The Tequila effect (Mexican crisis) • 47
    At the Commodity and Currency Exchange • 48
    My first futures • 52
    Riding the bull • 55
    The Asian Contagion • 57
    El Nino and Croesus • 59

4. The Russian Crisis • 62
    The new capitalist miracle • 62
    The crash • 64

      Worldwide turmoil • 67
      Greenspan saves the world • 69
      Thanksgiving and the Web • 72
      Bulgarian adventure • 75
5. The bubble • 77
      Brazil crisis • 77
      Dow 10,000! • 80
      Y2K-bug • 82
      Fait accompli • 85
      Final tech bubble • 87
      Disaster • 91
6. 2001 – A Bear Odyssey • 94
      My Finnish 'darling' • 94
      The Easter rally • 97
      Mathematics of the market: 2x2 = 5-1 • 99
      Profit warning • 101
      The falling knives • 103
      9/11 • 106
      The turning point • 109
      Marconi (Trade of the year) • 111
      The 'Taliban rally' • 113
7. Bottom fishing 116
      Put options experiment • 116
      Bull trap • 118
      Under the 'Osama lows' • 121
      Bargain hunting • 123
      The final US bottom • 127
      Bumpy ride • 129
      European capitulation • 131
      The Saddam turmoil • 133

8. Bull market again • 136
    The final European bottom • 136
    Fighting the trend • 138
    The bull is real! • 140
    Google • 142
    The emerging miracle • 144
    Forint and bonds • 148
    Compensation notes again • 151
    Oil vs. dollar • 153
    Where the sun never sets • 155

PART TWO: STORIES OF OTHER INVESTORS FROM THE TIME OF TRANSITION • 157

1. The Bond Trader • 159
2. The Journalist • 165
3. The Privatizer • 170
4. The 'Greedy' • 174
5. The Disciplined Trader • 177
6. The Gambler Genius • 181

PART THREE: A BEGINNER'S GUIDE TO THE STOCK MARKET • 185

1. Why do we need the stock exchange and how it works • 187
2. Valuation of stocks • 192
3. Other factors that influence the stock prices • 196

4. Trading techniques and instruments • 204
      Market cycles: when to buy? • 204
      When to sell: stop-loss and profit lock-in • 207
5. Technical analysis • 219

PART FOUR: STOCK MARKETS, INDICES, SHARES • 229

1. US Markets in general • 231
      A brief history of US markets • 232
      Indices and the manipulating of the Dow • 234
2. New York Stock Exchange • 237
3. NASDAQ • 243
      Bellwethers • 243
      Internet stocks • 245
      Semiconductor stocks • 249
      Others • 253
4. London Stock Exchange • 255
5. Deutsche Börse (German market) • 260
6. Other European shares in Amsterdam, Zurich, Paris and Helsinki • 265
7. Emerging Europe • 268
8. Russian shares • 272

Abbreviations • *277*
Glossary • *279*
Index • *283*

PROLOGUE

When someone asks me what I do as a profession, my answer is: I work with money, mainly at the stock market. Their next question is often how I started it. The answer isn't so simple; I usually start telling a long story. The person who took the question is listening to me as if I told an adventurous novel. And yes, it sounds like it! When I told it over and over again, I thought I should write it in a book, like a real novel. Maybe it is really as interesting!

At the same time, lots of people have told me they'd like to learn some basics about the stock market. Many of these people had tried buying stocks once or twice in recent years, usually trading on tips, or had simply been drawn to the market by the ever-rising prices in the late 1990s, only to realize that they knew nothing about the market. Now I've decided to publish this story of my adventures in the world of money, along with a basic overview of the stock market based on my own experience.

The first part tells the story of my adventures in the years of the transition from communism to the market economy in Eastern Europe, beginning in Hungary in the 1980s on street currency markets and continuing with my adventures with the East German mark, the Austrian schilling and other currencies. I then describe how I traded a variety of special equities and later went on to trade on the emerging stock markets in interesting times such as the Asian Contagion in 1997 and the Russian crisis in 1998. Finally I talk about how I began trading on the biggest world markets like the NYSE, the Nasdaq, and European markets, and my years of experience on these.

In the second part of the book, I recount the stories of some other traders whose careers took a more or less similar path to mine but each with its own unique and interesting aspect.

In the third part I explain the basics of the stock market in straight-forward terms and in the final part I also mention the most important markets and stocks which I traded.

During my career, I have relied on the experience of two famous stock market experts. One of them is Andre Kostolany, the speculator who operated on different markets for more than seven decades, and the other is Jesse Livermore, the trader king of the early 20th century. I quote from both of them several times.

I would recommend this book to anybody who is interested in adventurous stories about money, and anybody who has ever bought a stock or is planning to give it a try.

PART ONE:

The Story

1. MONEYMAKING AS A STUDENT

'Private import'

It's a sunny but chilly autumn day and we're having gym in the schoolyard. My best friend in the class runs up to me and says excitedly:
'Brezhnev is dead!'
'You're kidding, man.' – I said. I just couldn't believe it. The hard line Soviet leader had been in office for longer than I had been living, and it seemed he would remain in power forever... I thought my friend was just joking. He wasn't. And if we knew that the USSR would exist only less than another 10 years!

We lived in Budapest, the capital city of Hungary, where the political system was Soviet-style communism. Although it was more liberal than in other Eastern Bloc countries or the Soviet Union itself, everything depended on the Soviet leadership. In communist countries, where companies were all state-owned and equities markets had been closed for decades, things like stocks or bonds were unknown.

However, in the early 80s some institutions, mainly state-owned companies and local councils, were allowed to issue bonds, and from 1984, private investors were allowed to buy them in Hungary. The bonds paid 11% interest, much higher than the usual interest rates of 3-5% at that time. That was the first thing that drew my attention towards securities.

Even as a schoolboy, I remember reading about these bonds in a weekly economics magazine; I couldn't understand why the bonds paid such a high interest rate. The high yield attracted private and corporate money and the bonds were sold out in a short time, but there was no secondary market for them where prices could have gone up and this way yields could have gone down to their real value, where demand meets supply.

People were queuing for the bonds at the only bank that sold them, while some clever touts were buying and selling the bonds in front of the bank. As a teenage boy, of course I didn't have money to invest in these high yield bonds. I had to wait years, until after my first visit to the US. A friend of mine who worked in Budapest in a second-hand shop offered me a business opportunity when he heard that I would travel.

At that time, exports and imports, like almost everything else in the economy, was a state monopoly in communist countries. Instead of the market, the state decided what to import. It didn't import high-technology products, cosmetics, tropical fruits and a lot of other things. The only way of bringing them into the country was 'private import' by tourists. However, every person could travel to western (non-communist) countries only once in 3 years, so the prices of these items, imported by tourists, were high because of

Moneymaking as a student

the constant shortage of them. Second-hand shops bought these products from tourists and sold them to customers.

My friend suggested that I bring a video camera or a PC from the US. He said the shop would buy it from me at a high price. These were new products even in the US: the first generation of videos and personal computers, still unknown to most people. In the end after bargaining for weeks I bought a video camera in a small shop in West 10th Street in New York for a thousand dollars. The PC would have been too expensive; I didn't have enough money to buy it.

When I arrived home, my friend already had an end-user for the camera; he didn't even take it to the shop. I sold the camera direct to the buyer, and my friend took a commission from both of us. The profit was huge, almost 200%. I now had about three thousand dollars, which I wanted to invest immediately.

By that time, inflation and interest rates had been higher, but they were still in single-digit territory. Bonds still paid interest at 11% so the yield in real terms was not so huge any more, and as a result demand decreased. There were already enough bonds available, but still the same bank kept selling them. I went there; it was in the building where some years later the Stock Exchange reopened. I found a bond (issued by the state-owned rail company) that had 4.5 years until maturity; the price was 104% of the face value, which meant that the yield was even higher than 11%. I immediately bought it.

The issuing bank started to operate a secondary market for the bonds, but with not efficient market prices, so demand didn't really meet supply. Sometimes there was a lack of some bonds; other times there was an oversupply of others. Seeing this, the bank decided to open a real market about one year later. It was similar to a stock exchange, but it only opened once a week. There were still no brokers: anyone could go in and participate in the trading. At that time this didn't pose a problem; not more than fifty people turned up each week to trade bonds. The closing price of that day became the price at which the bank traded the bonds for a week, until the next market day.

My rail bonds rose from week to week. I was satisfied; I felt that I had made a good decision. But inflation continued rising, and a year later it stepped into double-digit territory. It meant that the yield of my bonds weren't any higher than the inflation rate so I sold them, still at a good price. I found another bond with a yield of 15% and about a year to maturity.

Escape to hard currencies

At the same time, another thing started to worry me about my investments. In 1986-87, the currency of my country, the forint, was devalued several times against the dollar and other currencies. In neighboring Poland I saw a dreadful example: their currency, the zloty, had been devalued to the point where it was practically worthless. I started to fear that the forint could go the same way and my investments would lose their value in dollar terms, so in 1988 I decided to sell my bonds and exchange my forints into dollars, West German marks and other strong currencies.

You would think nothing could be easier, but in reality, it was quite a difficult task! The forint was not a convertible currency; it couldn't legally be changed into other currencies except those of other communist countries. Money changing, like everything else, was a state monopoly, and the state suffered from a serious shortage of hard currencies.

I had no choice but to go to the black market. But I had to face two problems: black market prices were 50% higher than the official rate, and the market was primarily run by guys from the Middle East whom I was afraid might try to sell me counterfeit notes. So I was still trying to figure out how I could change my relatively small amount of forints into dollars or another hard currency at not much higher than the official rate. A friend of mine and I finally hit upon the solution. On a summer day, we started to offer foreign tourists the chance to exchange their currencies into forints at a rate that was a bit higher than the rate in the banks. We were still university students so to us it seemed like an adventure.

At first it wasn't easy: tourists were fed up with guys like us offering 'change' all the time. But after a while we found foreigners willing to exchange their money with us; it was part of their adventure in the Eastern

Bloc. The first hard currency I bought was a 500 Swiss franc note. To tell the truth, I had never seen such a banknote before; I didn't even know that such a high denomination existed. I was happy when I exchanged it for five 100-franc notes in a bank!

Later we bought mainly Austrian schillings and West German marks, but there were also US dollars, British pounds, Swedish and Danish crowns, Dutch guilders, French francs and Italian lira in our collection, depending on the nationality of the tourists. Of course a lot of these don't even exist any more; they were replaced by the euro.

By the end of October, we had managed to exchange half of our money. But in November, there were no tourists any more. Inflation was approaching 20% and there were wild rumors about a huge devaluation of the forint. We wanted to exchange our remaining forints before anything happened. I found the solution! I had heard a lot about the Austrian 'shopping tourism' in western Hungary, especially in Sopron, a town near the Austrian border and less than 50 miles from Vienna. The Austrians came there to buy all those products, mainly food, which were subsidized by the communist state and therefore incredibly cheap for them. I suggested to my friend that we go to Sopron and try it.

We went on a Friday afternoon. We didn't find the Austrians that evening, but the next morning we found our paradise: a department store full of Austrians! To our surprise, there were many other traders in front of the supermarket trying to exchange their schillings. At first we were a bit shy but later we became braver, and more importantly, successful. By the afternoon, we had run out of forints. We were so happy!

My friend didn't want to come again; he said he had enough schillings. I still had about a quarter of money in forints, so I decided to go alone. I went on December 8, an Austrian holiday; I was as successful as the first time. I went again still before Christmas and the work was done, my money was all in hard currencies! I felt I was saved. I had a lot of notes, colorful pieces, some of them beautiful.

Up until this moment my only goal had been to safeguard the value of my money, or perhaps add a little to it. But then I started thinking; I had bought the hard currencies at a good price, as far as I had forints. But I could buy more and maybe I could sell them at the much higher black market prices, so I could make money, not just preserve my capital. All I had to do was to find the buyers. I was still wary of doing business with black market traders on the street, so I decided to try to find the 'end-users'. These were people who traveled abroad, among them those who imported items like videos and PCs (like I had done earlier myself).

Polish markets and German tourists

However, the most important buyers were the street market vendors from Poland. After the collapse of the Polish currency, some items, mainly clothes, became very cheap in Poland, while others couldn't be bought at all. Because of this shortage, the black market rate of the hard currencies skyrocketed against the zloty, so the few goods that were available were quite cheap in terms of the dollar and other hard currencies. At the same time, millions of Poles lost their jobs; the only way to survive was selling these goods in foreign countries, on markets at the fringes of cities. The biggest Polish markets could be found in Mexico City and Singapore, and there was one in almost every Hungarian town; it was easy to find them.

I went to these markets, where the Poles sold their goods for forints, and then had to exchange them for dollars or West German marks. For these they received huge amounts of zloty, to buy more goods in Poland. They needed my dollars and marks, and they bought happily from me at a good rate. After a while, I found a great market in a small town; I went there about once or twice a week. As a student, I didn't have more time; speculation was only a part-time job...

When I had sold almost all of my hard currency, I counted my money. It was in forints again, but it was 50% more than before I had converted it all into hard currency! The possibility of devaluation didn't worry me any more. I thought I would be able to buy and sell currencies and make money continuously.

In the first months of 1989, we went to Sopron to buy schillings, and then on to the Polish markets to sell dollars and German marks. The Poles preferred dollars and marks, so we changed our schillings into these currencies in the bank. Hard currencies could be legally exchanged for other hard currencies; only the forint and other 'eastern' currencies remained officially unconvertible.

The cheap Polish currency provided excellent holiday opportunities as well: we could go skiing in Poland for about $15 a week. And on one occasion, we bought air tickets for the Krakow-Warsaw-Berlin-Prague-Budapest route for $4-$5 altogether! Airfares between communist countries were dirt cheap, especially if we paid for them in zloty; all we had to do was travel to Poland and buy the tickets there. I met guys who had bought air tickets for destinations like Cuba, Mongolia and North Korea for as little as $15-$20!

In the summer, when there were lots of tourists, the supply of hard currencies increased and black market prices dropped. The profit gap narrowed, so we wanted to buy as much hard currency as we could. In order to collect cheap West German marks, we headed to the tourist paradise of Germans at Lake Balaton. It was one of the few places where East and West Germans could meet each other during the long decades when Germany was divided. East Germans were allowed to travel to five countries only: Poland, Czechoslovakia, Hungary, Romania and Bulgaria. Of these, the West Germans preferred Hungary because it was relatively cheap for them and more goods and services were available, compared to the others. The East Germans brought their worthless East German marks, the West Germans their strong marks.

Adventurous moneymaking

We went to campsites, pitched our tent and went to the beach. In the early evening, when the Germans returned to their tents and caravans, we took our forints and went round the campsite, asking the West Germans if they wanted to exchange marks for forints. Most of them changed money with us happily, and some of them even came to our tent when they wanted to change more. There were some Dutch and Danish tourists as well who exchanged their guilders and crowns with the same enthusiasm. But the poor East Germans, we had to avoid them. Little did we know that the following summer the situation would be reversed and we'd be searching them out!

At the end of that summer in 1989, many of the East Germans didn't want to go home. They stayed, and more and more came after them. They started hoping that the Hungarian government would open the border for them so that they could move to West Germany. In September, their dream came true; the borders were opened. Two months later Berlin Wall came down and Germans could travel and meet each other in their homeland. The communist system soon collapsed. In Hungary and Poland it happened peacefully, in Prague and Berlin in a more revolutionary way, and at last in Romania, brutally.

Western tourists avoided the region in that revolutionary autumn so there was no more currency to buy. I held onto my hard currencies and sold them in the winter, when the black-market price was 50% higher than the official one. I knew from my experience the previous year that this gap would be narrowing in the summer when the tourists came back, so in the spring I kept my savings in forints; I wasn't afraid of devaluation any more.

We still didn't know what would take the place of communism. In those early days it wasn't yet obvious that the same capitalist, free market system would be put in place as in the West. The Soviet Union would still exist for another two years.

The East German mark

The Germans wanted to be unified quickly; they still feared that the USSR might change its policy. Rumors started to emerge about the union of the two German currencies. I never thought that the worthless East German mark would be converted to Deutschmark at a good rate. I thought the Germans would do what they had done in West Germany in 1948, when each person got 40 D-Marks (West German marks) and could throw away their old Reichsmarks. So I didn't believe that the East German mark might be worth buying, but one day in early 1990, the exchange rate, which was then about 1:8, started to rise in Berlin and Vienna. Somebody clearly knew something!

In Hungary, currencies of former communist countries could still be exchanged at rates set by the state. These rates were only changed about once a year, so the East German mark remained quite low. I started to buy as much as I could, and took it to Vienna to change into schillings, which were pegged to the D-Mark. To my surprise, in front of the bank in Vienna some Slavic guys, I thought they might have been Serbs, stopped me and asked if I had any eastern currency to change. I said I had East German marks, and they invited me to a shop on Mexikoplatz where I negotiated with a middle-aged guy who might have been Russian or Armenian. He offered me a good price and I said OK, without bargaining. The deal was done!

I returned to Budapest, exchanged the schillings into forints, and promptly bought more East German marks. The next day when I called the bank in Vienna, I learned that the rate of the East German mark had fallen, so I immediately sold mine to someone who still wanted to buy in Budapest. In another few days, the rate rallied again in Vienna. I wanted to buy East German marks again, but there were none available any more. The bank clerks had taken them themselves to Vienna, even to West Berlin, and made a huge profit.

In the meantime currency unification became a reality. The Germans announced the details: each East German citizen could put all their money into a special account, which would be converted into D-Marks on July 1 at a rate of 1:1 for the first 4000 marks and 1:2 for anything above that.

In the middle of June I found a Hungarian bank advertising that they had East German marks available. I called the banks in Vienna and Berlin on the phone, but they didn't buy any more. I thought it was all over. I was wrong: the guy on Mexikoplatz was still buying East German marks, almost until the last day. Maybe they had found a way to put the money into the accounts of East German citizens and get it back for a small profit after it had been converted into D-Marks. In any case, it was a big mistake for me not to try Mexikoplatz: I could have taken all the East German marks that remained in Hungarian banks there.

After July 1, some East Germans headed to Lake Balaton just as they'd done in years past, except now they had the strong D-Marks and were getting 50 forints to the mark, compared to just 7 forints just a month earlier. They must have felt like they were in heaven. And of course, they were very pleased when we offered them even a little more for their new money. We bought far more marks from them than we'd ever bought from the West Germans! Now we avoided the West Germans and preferred the East Germans with their old bangers, Trabants and Wartburgs. I thought this heaven would last for years.

That same summer I spent a month at the National Bank of Hungary as a junior consultant. It was an interesting experience to see the currency market at the highest level there and the lowest level on the black market at the same time.

My first steps on the stock market

The same year, 1990, an important institution of the fledgling capitalist system, the Stock Exchange, was opened in Budapest. The first listed stock, IBUSZ (a travel agency) skyrocketed on the very first day, from 5,000 to 12,000 forints (or about $60 to $140), but it was only a one-day miracle. From there the share price started to fall slowly. When it reached 8,000 forints, or a third cheaper than its peak price, I thought it was a bargain and bought three shares. Not a thousand, not a hundred – only three shares. Luckily for me not more, as it turned out. I bought into the falling knives: the price of the stock continued to fall. A few months later I decided to cut my losses, selling my three shares at 5,000 forints, which was just as well: over the next few years, IBUSZ fell all the way to 300 forints, or about $3 at the exchange rate of the time.

This small-scale foray into the stock market taught me a valuable lesson, namely that a stock isn't necessarily a bargain just because its price has fallen considerably. To tell the truth I didn't know much about things like stock valuation; I just wanted to try stock trading and this was the first, fortunately low, tuition fee I would have to pay as I learned my way around the market.

The Stock Exchange was a small room divided into two parts in a new office building. One part was the trading floor, with only 10-12 brokers trading by open outcry. The other part was for visitors and journalists; a rope separated the two parts. The trading lasted only an hour every day.

My second stock, in a brewery, made me a little profit, about 5%. The third one was Fotex, the first of the newly emerging private Hungarian enterprises (later listed on the New York Stock Exchange). When it came on the market at a price of 199 forints (only about $3) a share, it seemed so favorable that I planned to buy as much as I could. Demand was so heavy that people were queuing up to and I only managed to get a fraction of the shares I had planned to buy. I thought Fotex would open about 50% higher on the Stock Exchange, but it opened only 10% higher and then slipped back almost to the issue price. I sold it with a small profit.

At that point I decided the market was not worth trading on, so this was my last stock purchase for a long time. The Budapest Stock Exchange was still too small, with not enough stocks and liquidity, and prices were falling or stagnating. It was a young market; it needed time to develop. And this poor baby market was only a month and half old when Saddam Hussein invaded Kuwait. Investors escaped from all the world markets, and the price of oil suddenly surged to an all-time high. Under these circumstances, who would have bought stocks in such a fledgling market?

In the first year of trading, 10 or 12 stocks were listed in Budapest. Most of them were listed in Vienna at the same time, and Austrian investors started to buy them, convinced by brokers that these were bargain shares of companies in their new capitalist neighbour. But they weren't. These shares, mainly in smaller companies that were among the first to be privatized, had their initial public offerings at high prices. Overvalued from the beginning, most of them fell to a fraction of the original offering price.

'Shopping tourism' in Austria

I was still a university student; nothing urged me to trade stocks and I returned to the currency market. Traveling to Vienna with the East German marks earlier, I had noticed that there was a strong demand for the forint in Austria. A lot of Hungarians traveled there, mainly to go shopping. It was still only a year after the collapse of communism and some goods, like electronic household appliances were still not available in Hungary, so lots of people traveled for them to nearby Austria, the only 'old' capitalist neighbouring country. These people needed schillings, but changing forints for convertible currencies was still not officially allowed in Hungary so they had to exchange them in Austria, where the exchange rate was very bad.

I had an excellent idea: I went to the biggest shopping malls, and suggested to the Hungarian shoppers there that they change their forints into schillings at a better rate than in the banks in Austria. This way I could sell the German marks I had bought at Lake Balaton at an excellent price (marks could be changed to schillings in Austria; the two currencies were pegged to each other). In the autumn of 1990, I could sell schillings this way at even higher rates than on the black market in Hungary, but I couldn't buy again because fewer and fewer Austrians were going to Sopron. The Hungarian state had stopped subsidizing goods and they weren't so cheap any more.

Instead, I decided to try buying hard currencies from the people who ran the black market. As I had feared, this turned out to be a bad idea. Once I bought 1000 German marks (fortunately it wasn't a bigger amount) but as we were doing the deal, other fellows appeared and they robbed me.

After this shock, I had to find a more secure way to buy schillings or marks, as long as I could continue to sell them at such a high price. Then something occurred to me: if the guy on Mexikoplatz in Vienna had changed East German marks at a good rate, why wouldn't he change forints at a good rate? I was right; he was glad to see me again and changed my forints at a reasonable price. Then I took the schillings to the shopping malls, sold them to the Hungarians and took the forints back to Mexikoplatz. Often other students made the trip with me, and while I was busy exchanging money, they went shopping or walked around in Vienna; it was a good laugh for all of us.

In early 1991, the black market price of western currencies against the forint fell back to the official level. The reason: Hungary had become a capitalist economy, where importing and exporting goods became free. There was no more shortage of goods; 'private import' by tourists became unnecessary. At the same time demand for consumer goods dropped suddenly, as a result of the high unemployment that followed the collapse of the old communist industry. Supply and demand finally began to balance each other out as they do in every market economy, even if at a low level. The forint became a stable and convertible currency and the black market disappeared.

The Czechoslovakian crown

Around this time, I discovered one more excellent arbitrage opportunity on the currency market: the rate of the Czechoslovakian crown was a few percent higher in Vienna than in Budapest. A friend of mine and I started to buy crowns in Budapest and take them to Mexikoplatz, to my old friend from the days of the East German mark. In the winter, when Hungarians traveled to nearby Slovakia for skiing and needed crowns, the situation changed and the rate became higher in Budapest, so we went to Vienna, bought crowns there, and sold them in Hungary. This situation changed four or five times; we carried the green 100 'Korun' (the Slovak name of the currency) notes from one city to the other, whichever way we could get the higher rate.

On Mexikoplatz we felt nostalgia: Andre Kostolany had traded the same currencies in the same place 70 years earlier, in the turmoil that followed the break-up of the Austro-Hungarian Monarchy. At that time, he was trading the new and volatile Hungarian, Austrian and Czechoslovak currencies; now we were trading the same currencies in the transition period that followed the break-up of communism. Some of these countries and their currencies that had been new 70 years earlier, now soon disappeared themselves. Czechoslovakia, Yugoslavia, and the Soviet Union, were gone from the map, along with my beloved Czechoslovakian crown. The currencies of the new countries soon became convertible; there were no more trading opportunities.

In the end of 1991, I found one last opportunity arising from the 'shopping tourism' in Austria (which I kicked myself for not finding earlier). Like in every country, those who purchased goods and took them abroad for consumption could claim back the VAT (or *Mehrwertsteuer* in German) in Austria. This meant that all the Hungarians who went shopping in Austria could claim a rebate. They had to show the goods at customs on the border, the customs officer stamped their rebate forms, and when they came to Austria next time, they could go back to the shop to collect their money. Banks also paid it, but they charged a fee of about 30% of the total. However, most people didn't plan to return to Austria very soon, and it was difficult to find the small bank on the border. Most of them, traveling by coach, didn't even have time for it because the driver would be urging them to get back home as fast as possible.

That was where I came in: I stood near Austrian customs and offered people the sum they would get in a bank, that is about 70% of the total VAT. Most said yes, I paid them, collected their rebate forms and then went to the shops myself, where I received the full sum. (I only did business when the shop was in or around Vienna.) Everybody was satisfied: the people received the same VAT rebate they would have gotten at a bank, and I collected the profit instead of the banks. As many people wouldn't have returned to Austria to claim their rebates within a year's time and would have lost their money, it was a win-win situation. But this business didn't last long. As the market economy took off in Hungary, more and more supermarkets and shopping malls were opened and people didn't have to travel abroad for shopping any more.

This eventful period of my life, with its traveling, currency trading and so many other adventures, was finally over. During this time, the unbelievable came true: communism was gone and freedom and the capitalism had arrived (a bit wildly at first, it was true). I had gained a lot of experience, and of course, made a nice sum of money, enough in fact to start trading equities, a new adventure which began with another opportunity unique to the transitional economies of the former communist countries.

2. THE COMPENSATION NOTE

The idea

One day I read an article about 'compensation' in the same weekly magazine where I had found the high-rate bonds seven years earlier. I immediately knew it was my next opportunity. That was the time I graduated from university and faced a dilemma: should I get a job, or should I continue speculation full time? As I read the article about compensation notes, I decided on the latter.

The first democratically elected Hungarian government wanted to compensate all those people whose property had been taken by the communist state and those who went to jail for political reasons under fascist and communist rule. The young democratic state didn't have the funds needed to offer money as compensation. Instead, they issued compensation notes that could be exchanged for state property during privatization, a process that included land, shops and restaurants, and shares of companies.

The state paid interest on the compensation notes for 3 years, from 1991. This interest was not paid in cash; instead, it was added to the face value of the notes. In this way, by 1994 the 'official' value of the note had grown to 174% of the face value, where it has remained ever since. Under the original plan, the whole process was to be completed during this three-year period, but ten years later it was still not completely finished.

So people got printed securities with a face value, and they didn't know what to do with them. They wanted money, of course the face value of the note. They didn't care about the interest; they just wanted to get the sum that was printed on it. But who needed the notes?

The state started to privatize smaller companies right away. Buyers were allowed to pay a part of the price with compensation notes, which the state accepted at the official rate, adjusted to include any interest that had accrued. This meant it was only worth buying the notes for under face value, and later even over it but still well under 174%. The owners would have dumped their notes at or a bit under the face value; in the end supply and demand met each other at 70%.

There were several hundred thousand people willing to sell small quantities of the notes, and only a few end-users seeking big quantities. Someone had to collect the notes. The banks and brokerage firms weren't ready for this task, and they didn't want to invest in such a temporary thing. The market needed flexible entrepreneurs, and I saw my opportunity. My girlfriend and I decided to organize it. When I saw in some daily newspapers that some brokerage firms had placed a bid for the notes, we started to collect them immediately. First we went to the office where people received the notes and simply asked them if they wanted to sell them. Some of them said yes, and we bought the first packages at 70%. Then we started to advertise in the daily newspaper that we would buy the notes. Soon we opened an office in Budapest, and later in other towns as well.

We sold the collected notes to brokerage firms, who had orders from end-users but were only interested in buying large quantities. In the first few weeks it was easy; we could make a profit of 5 percent between the buying and selling price. In a few months, other traders emerged and the competition meant that the profit margin narrowed to about 1-2 percent. This wasn't much, but still enough to make it worthwhile.

At the same time, the state privatization agency offered shares of companies for compensation notes as well. The first one was the travel agency IBUSZ, which was the first stock I had speculated with two years earlier. Shares were going for 2,500 forints on the market (if you remember, I had sold my first shares at 5,000 forints a share), but if you bought notes on the market and exchanged them for IBUSZ shares, you could get the shares for about 2,200. Of course I changed notes into shares and sold them immediately on the Stock Exchange. The issued shares sold out quickly, so this business was soon over.

In the meantime, we were buying notes from more and more places in the country. People traveled to us from everywhere. In the mornings, I went to the railway stations to meet them and buy their notes, then during the day we collected notes from people who came to the office, and in the evenings, we met some guys who collected notes in other cities and sold them to us. Business was booming!

The Mafia

Some days we traveled to other cities to collect notes ourselves. On one occasion, in a city in southwest Hungary, the local note-traders formed a mafia and tried to force us out of town. We didn't have an office there so we met people willing to sell their notes in a post office at the railway station.

On one occasion, when we arrived the mafia of local traders were already there, offering 2% more for the notes. I told them we would offer even more. I was sure we could offer at least as much as they could. When they realized this, they became embarrassed. Then I suggested that we pay the original price to the sellers and divide the notes we could buy equally. They agreed to this, but we were hardly able to buy anything. To tell the truth, these were ugly guys and they frightened people so I think most people decided not to do business with them. I asked them why they hadn't called us on the phone (they could read the phone number in the ad) and said that it was their city and we weren't welcome there. We would have accepted their point of view and we'd have left the city. I guess they thought they could frighten us away if only we met them and saw how aggressive guys they were.

The compensation note

As we had already put one more ad in the local newspaper for the next week, we made a deal with them that we would collect the notes from whoever called us after that ad and then leave. They didn't keep their word: they directed us to false addresses by calling up and pretending to be note holders willing to sell. However, we still managed to collect so many notes from real sellers on that last tour so we were quite satisfied.

Then we moved on to a neighboring city, and opened an office there. It was a gold mine: there was no other buyer in that city! I traveled there every second or third day to collect the notes personally. It was a nice time in my life: I traveled and organized a lot, got to talk to a lot of people, and made good money.

From late 1992, the compensation note was listed on the Stock Exchange. From then on, everybody looking at the stock market news could see the price, but note holders didn't want to sell on the Exchange because they would have had to open an account, give an order, and wait for their money until the settlement was done. Most of them had only a few notes so the relative cost of selling them through the Stock Exchange would have been high. It was easier for them to sell us or to other buyers a few percent under the Stock Exchange price. The brokerage firms liked to buy outside the Exchange too, so that they didn't push up the price there if they had a big order.

Around the end of the year, there was heavy demand for the notes due to a big privatization deal. The price kept going up from about 70 to 80 and business was great. As had happened so many times earlier, I thought this would last forever. On New Year's Eve, on a skiing trip in Czechoslovakia, I was optimistically looking forward to the year ahead at the very moment when the country broke up into the Czech Republic and Slovakia. My good old friend the Czechoslovakian crown was replaced by two new currencies, but who cared when I had such a fine new friend in the compensation note?

Note speculation

In the first days of 1993, note buyers suddenly disappeared. I couldn't believe it. The price slipped to about 70% of the face value, but the market dried up. We stopped buying for a while, and during this dry spell, we lost our whole note-delivering network. They urged us to keep buying, still at a good price, but we couldn't find a market for the notes so we had to refuse them. Our stronger competitor in Budapest kept buying even without any profit, just to keep their market share.

After two months like this, I was considering closing the whole business when a brokerage firm gave us an order for a large quantity of notes at a fixed price for one week. The fixed price was a bit higher than the actual market price, so it was easier to collect; the competitors couldn't grant the higher price. There was of course a risk: if the price rose sharply in the meantime,

The compensation note

or we couldn't buy enough notes, we would have to buy at the last minute at any price. But this problem never occurred. For the brokerage firm it was a good solution as well: they sold the collected notes to the end-user at a good price and didn't have to worry about actually collecting them; that was our job. As they were satisfied with our work, the firm soon placed another, bigger order with us. Our self-confidence returned, and seeing our relatively high bids, new suppliers called us to offer their notes, one of them from the city where the mafia had tried to run us out, which I viewed as a personal victory.

After this, the price of the note became volatile, as demand would increase suddenly after someone won a privatization auction and then disappear when the buyer got the quantity he needed. Supply remained strong as the Compensation Office issued more and more notes. By this time, I had enough money to exploit this volatility. When brokers called and urged us to sell them notes, I knew they must have a big order and I was sure they would push up the price with their bids so we wouldn't sell the notes immediately. Instead we held onto them for a few days, only selling when the price was a few percent higher.

In the summer, there was an interesting case. One of our suppliers, a young guy from the city of Pecs, went on holiday. His mother called us desperately on a Friday morning and said that a lot of note holders were waiting there to sell, but she couldn't do anything without her son. We took as much cash as we could and went down. We arrived early that evening to find a lot of people already waiting for us. We bought all of their notes and then went around to different addresses of other people who had called earlier, willing to sell.

We stayed in Pecs that night and continued buying the next morning until we ran out of cash. We didn't sell this enormous quantity of notes immediately. There was a rally, so we waited a week and earned an extra 10%.

On the way home, we stopped off in the city where we had had the monopoly the previous year. Again we saw that nobody was buying notes there, so we decided at once to retake the city for our 'empire'. In no time it became a gold mine for us once again. We employed a retired cashier there who could handle the cash as well as the notes, and I traveled there every second or third day for almost a year to collect the notes. On the train, I often read the *Financial Times* and *The Wall Street Journal*, as I was more and more interested in international finances.

It was the first time I heard the expression 'emerging markets' to refer to the markets in places like Mexico, Argentina, Brazil, Turkey, and countries in Southeast Asia. Sometimes the articles also mentioned the former European communist countries with their young markets as future possibilities, but big institutional buyers were still not really interested and without them, the three-year-old Budapest Stock Exchange was dull, with little volume and flat prices.

Back to the stock market

In the second half of 1993, the privatization agency started to offer more stocks in exchange for the compensation notes. The first one to go on sale was Pick, the famous salami maker. There was high demand for the shares and those who bought shares in the initial issue made a huge profit in a short time. From then onwards investors started buying notes, in the expectation that the next issues would be as profitable as Pick had been. This meant that we could sell the notes not only to the brokerage companies, but directly to the investors as well. It was the best situation imaginable for us: sellers and buyers were queuing up in front of our office.

Because of the anticipated profits, demand was high for the new offerings and as a result each investor got only a few shares. Some clever speculators collected several hundred people, mainly university students, gave them notes, and sent them to buy the new issues. Each received a few shares, the speculators collected these from them (giving the students a small sum for their 'work'), and in this way the speculators amassed several hundred or thousand shares, which they could sell for 100% profit or more.

I had enough business so I didn't participate in this using-students-to-get-cheap-shares scheme. However, there were two occasions when there were no queues for the newly issued shares. (Maybe the students got tired by the end of the year.) These were the shares of

Adventurous moneymaking

a natural gas company and a furniture retail company. I bought a lot of each before Christmas.

In the first days of 1994, I rushed to the Stock Exchange to see how my two stocks were performing. The Stock Exchange was now in a nice building, with the trading floor in an enormous room and there I saw something I had never seen before during the whole three and a half-year history of that young market: prices started to rise, day by day. Seeing the higher prices, I sold my stocks. What a mistake! The bull market was just beginning.

Trading was still done by open outcry. The demand was so strong, that every day when trading started, every broker shouted at the same moment, 'I would buy this and that share!' There was only one thin voice shouting, 'I'm selling!' It was impossible to decide who the buyer was; usually the tallest and strongest broker would win. For about a month there was a real fight for the stocks and during this time the market index doubled, and some stocks tripled in value. When the fast bull run was over – exactly on February 2, when the bear is coming out of its cave for the first time – every broker was shouting, 'Sell!', and now there was a fight for selling every day.

What had caused this fast and furious bull run? As I mentioned, there was a strong bull market on the emerging markets in 1993, and that spread to the freshly discovered markets of the former Eastern Bloc countries in January 1994. From that point, the third world and former communist (second world) countries were lumped together in one big group, the 'emerging markets'.

Later that year, electronic trading took place on the Stock Exchange, but at first in a somewhat funny way: 24 of the 40-50 listed shares were separated into three groups containing eight shares each. There was only 20 minutes for trading in each group electronically, and the remaining stocks were still traded by open outcry.

The OTC market

The stock market became dull again after that first and fast bull run and was still for almost two years. However, there was another interesting sector of the market outside the Exchange. A lot of companies had only been partially privatized, and the shares of these companies were still not listed on the Stock Exchange. The owners of these shares still wanted to trade them, so an Over the Counter (OTC) market emerged.

In 1994, the state privatization agency offered some shares for compensation notes again, but these shares weren't listed on the Stock Exchange immediately (in fact, some of them were never listed). After the big January bull, investors thought that the only stocks worth buying for notes were those that would soon come onto the Exchange so they didn't rush for the others. This proved to be a mistake. The Stock Exchange was still not sophisticated, so if a big fund decided to buy shares, they didn't mind buying at OTC as well.

This way there were some shares available for notes that weren't very popular among local investors, some of which were very cheap fundamentally (with a P/E ratio of 2 or 3!). As they were so cheap and I could get as many as I wanted for my notes, I decided to buy them. One of them was a pharmaceutical company, Chinoin. I made a 100% profit on it in three months, and that was just the beginning; in the next two years it rose another 200 percent. As it turned out, the French pharmaceutical company Sanofi was buying the shares, until in the end they got all of them.

Another company that interested me was MOL, an oil and gas company, the former state monopoly. I was sure that sooner or later some of the big oil companies would be interested in buying into it, and I was right. The price of one share was one compensation note with a face value of 1000 forints. As the price of the note was 60% at that time, I could buy the MOL shares for 600 forints. The planned issuing period was two weeks, but it was closed after four days. Small investors didn't really buy many shares, but on the fourth day, someone bought all of the remaining shares. That could only be a big institution!

As I saw my theory proved, I decided to add to my stock on the OTC market after the issue. I expected to get shares for about 750 forints, but the demand was so strong that the best price I could buy was at 840. I continued buying shares all the way up to 1000 forints. I liked the OTC market because there were nice trends, without wild price movements. I could sleep much bet-

The compensation note

ter, even keeping giant quantities of OTC stocks, than when I had stocks listed on the Exchange.

I was so confident, that – for the first time in my life – I decided to buy on margin as well. It wasn't as easy as it is today. First of all, brokerage companies still didn't trade on margin. The stocks were still printed papers; I had to take them to a bank that was willing to grant credit on the stocks as a margin. The bank gave cash, and I took the cash to the brokerage firms where I bought more stocks, usually after bargaining. This way I continued buying MOL shares at 1000-1020 forints, and the price kept rising to around 1100.

I kept my shares until September, when one day I saw sharply lower prices among the bids of the brokerage companies. I didn't want to risk the huge profit, so I immediately sold all my shares at 1070. The price fell further, but it never got under 1000 forints again.

Meanwhile the compensation note business started to fade. There was less and less demand and the price slowly slipped to 50% of the face value. In the summer of 1994, the second free elections took place in the country. The new government viewed the compensation note scheme as a mistake of the first freely elected government, so they ignored it for about a year and as demand decreased, the price kept dropping. The state had issued more notes than could be used and the price tumbled, down to a point where people were not willing to sell. The market gradually dried up. Volume was little, costs were high and the competition strong, so I found it wasn't worth buying notes any more. The only place I kept buying was my faithful city, where I was the only buyer. The office there worked and made a moderate profit, though they could buy only small amounts. All I had to do was travel there once a week. But when the price slipped below 30%, I gave that last office to my note-collecting friend. Who knows, maybe he would still be running the office today, if our cashier hadn't finally retired.

The beautiful two years dominated by the compensation note were over. Although the scheme was originally designed to last for only three years, I made some trades with the note as late as in 2003, as we will see. Who would have thought that it would still exist more than a decade after it was created? And even after all this, I started investing in Bulgarian compensation notes...

3. THE WAY TO SOPHISTICATED MARKETS

The Tequila effect (Mexican crisis)

By the autumn, the prices on the Budapest Stock Exchange fell back almost to the level they had been before the January rally. As was the case for so many other investors, I kept them cheap. This time I made a certain mistake traders often do: I bought *just because* prices had fallen so much. I didn't examine the technical condition of the market carefully. Had prices been much higher, it would have meant that the market was strong. But prices fell back to levels where they started rising, and at the end of the year, they fell even further. I sold some shares as soon as I saw they didn't perform well (using the stop-loss for the first time), which was a good decision. At the same time, my beloved MOL skyrocketed on the OTC market. I could hardly jump on it between 1100 and 1200 forints and in another few days, it had soared up to 1400.

    One day in early 1995, I read about the financial problems plaguing Mexico. The country had run out of currency reserves and the Mexican peso had to be devalued: it fell to half its value within weeks. President Clinton rushed to help his southern neighbor; the US wanted to avoid a bigger Mexican crisis with millions of refugees at almost any price. In all, Clinton organized a relief package of about 50 billion dollars for Mexico.

At first I didn't really care about the Mexican crisis. But after a while, analysts started mentioning it as the 'Tequila effect', which could spread to other markets, first of all Moscow and Budapest. That time the Hungarian economy was really struggling and the current account deficit was increasing fast. It was too much for me: I immediately sold my MOL shares at 1350 forints. The Tequila effect soon reached the stock: within weeks it had fallen to 1000 forints.

In February, the Finance Minister and the President of the Central Bank resigned in Hungary. I sold my remaining two stocks on the Stock Exchange, at a huge loss. And I did something I hadn't been doing for quite a long time: fearing that the forint could go the way of the peso, I changed my forints into German marks and US dollars.

At the Commodity and Currency Exchange

In March we had a new Finance Minister and Central Bank President. Everybody expected a kind of shock therapy in the economy, beginning with the devaluation of the forint. However, investors these days didn't have to go to the black market any more if they wanted to buy other currencies, or in other words sell the forint short. They could do it at the Commodity Exchange, which had opened a bit later than the Stock Exchange. Wheat, corn and other agricultural products could be traded there, and there was a booming currency section as well.

The currency section became popular in 1994, when the US dollar fell fast against the Japanese yen and the German mark: from 1.70-1.80 to as low as 1.28 marks, the lowest level since the birth of the Deutschmark in 1948. Of course, lots of traders started speculating on these currencies. Generally, at every market, big moves attract the traders, and this was no exception.

Now the investors sold the forint short, especially on the March expiry, expecting a shock therapy, first of all a huge devaluation from the new financial government. I didn't join them because I thought the government would wait until the expiry had passed and then devalue the forint. I was wrong. Two days before the expiry, the shock therapy was launched with a 10% immediate devaluation, so the traders got their reward, many insiders among them, I suppose.

Alongside this 10%, the government started devaluing the forint on continuous basis, little by little every day, at a rate of about 14% a year against a basket which consisted of 70% German mark and 30% US dollar. In this way, future rates could be calculated. Another element of the package was the government's decision to pay high interest rates on treasury bonds, in order to attract foreign capital. At the top end in 1995, these rates were as high as 35% (with inflation reaching the same level at that time).

This meant that difference between the forint and dollar/mark interest rates was huge, much higher than the rate of devaluation, which could be calculated in advance. It provided an excellent arbitrage opportunity for foreign investors and domestic traders as well. They sold marks and dollars short against the forint, in the ratio of the basket, at the futures prices. These futures prices were determined by the difference between the forint interest rate and that of the two currencies, which was as high as about 28-30%, while the actual currency exchange rates in the future (the devaluation of the forint) was only 14%. The margin requirement was small, so a hundred percent profit could easily be reached.

An example: Let's say one dollar was 100 forints, one mark 70 forints on a given day. The interest rate of the two currencies was an average of 4%, while the forint interest rate for one year was 30%. The difference is 26%, it means the futures prices for one year expiry are that higher (126 forints for the dollar, 88 forints for the mark). The investors sold the two currencies short against the forint at these prices. At the expiry, the prices were 114 forints for the dollar and 80 forints for the mark (devalued by 14% in a year). This meant a profit of 12 forint for one dollar and 8 forints for one mark. The margin requirement was about 10 forints for a contract, so it means about a hundred percent, without any serious risk.

It seemed like a good, risk-free opportunity and it really was, but only for a short time. I spent a longer period of time in Britain, so I discovered it only in the summer of that year. Others who had started sooner got rich quickly.

As soon as it had privatized the biggest companies and thus acquired enough foreign capital, the government lowered the rates; it didn't need the 'hot' money anymore, which was flying from country to country seeking such high profits. Interest rates and the level of devaluation soon fell into single-digit territory.

Later, in 1996, I tried trading wheat and corn. Prices were at historical highs both in Budapest and in Chicago. I expected a fall, and sold both wheat and corn short. I was right, but first I was squeezed: prices rose higher before they collapsed and that squeezed me out of my position.

Meanwhile, the Budapest Stock Exchange became more sophisticated. There was now fully computerized stock trading; only the newly opened futures section was traded by open outcry. It was still fun to watch: the brokers shouted their bids and offers so loud that they simply couldn't hear properly if somebody called them on the phone to give an order.

There was a visitor's gallery in the Stock Exchange where we could stay all day long. I met a lot of interesting people; a few of them I'm still friends with today. I also met journalists, and one day one of them asked me if I would write an article about currency markets for an economic daily. I wrote it, and they asked me to write more. I started to write about the stock market, the futures market and also about the compensation notes. Later I wrote for some weekly magazines as well. I've been a freelance journalist ever since.

My first futures

In late 1995, the longest ever bull market was in its 13th year in the US. That was the time it started to become a bubble – or 'irrational exuberance', as Greenspan named it. We can see it on the chart of the S&P 500 in Figure 2, page 190: it had risen slowly to 500 points and then started rising much more steeply in '95. Funds and individual investors rediscovered emerging markets, now including those of the former Eastern Bloc as well. These countries were developing fast, their economies growing at 5% per year or more. In Central and Eastern Europe, privatization was almost over and capitalism was starting to work efficiently, but stocks were still undervalued. Shares of good and growing companies were available with P/E ratios as low as 6-8, numbers last seen on Wall Street at the end of the 1973-74 bear market. Emerging market funds and other institutions, mainly from the US, bought into these bargains.

In the last days of 1995 prices started skyrocketing and never looked back. There were only small corrections, followed by even bigger rises. The benchmark of the Stock Exchange, the BUX, was 1600 points in late 1995, and had risen to 9000 in just 18 months! It was one of the biggest and fastest rallies I've ever seen on a single market, even bigger than the tech bubble on the Nasdaq in 1999-2000. The leaders were pharmaceutical companies, just like on other markets. The most successful was Richter, which had risen 150% by the summer, 500% by the end of the year, and 1000% by April 1997! Other sectors performed well too, and there were hardly any stocks that didn't rise several hundred percent in 1996.

After five years of a dull, sideways market, I didn't believe that the bull market would last long. The only bullish period I had seen was the furious 1-month rally two years earlier. Newcomers to the stock market didn't have such experience, and they bought shares happily. I bought and sold stocks and futures, but made only a small profit. Of course I should have bought and sat tight; in a bull market, that's the way to make money, by sitting tight, not by jumping in and out.

Around this time I started to trade futures, mainly for the index of the market, the BUX (Budapest Stock Index). As I knew there was a bull market, I almost always opened long positions, but, unfortunately, I soon closed them with a moderate profit when I should have kept them until expiry.

One day I ran into a guy I knew from the compensation note business; he had collected notes around Lake Balaton and sold them to me. He told me about another guy who had 300 contracts of long BUX (the open interest were 1000 contracts)!

A few days later when the finance minister of the previous year's stabilization resigned, there was a market pullback, a heavy correction. There was panic in the visitors' gallery, and I heard a guy shouting, 'Sell 100 contracts!' I asked him his name and realized he was the investor my friend had mentioned. He asked me how I knew his name and I told him that he already had a reputation. He told me that he had only 200 contracts, not 300, but even that was 20 percent of the open interest! We started talking, and have been friends ever since.

The panic lasted only that day. The new finance minister had a good reputation and continued the policy of his predecessor. The bull market went on as if nothing had happened.

In mid 1996 we discovered that the Budapest Stock Exchange was in correlation with Wall Street and other big markets such as the London Stock Exchange and the Deutsche Börse (German Stock Exchange). It was natural, as Hungary got into the bloodstream of the world economy and the same money supplied its stock market, the same funds, investment banks, the global capital.

The Dow Jones Industrial Average stood at about 5000 points at that time. In a few months, we heard Greenspan's famous speech about 'irrational exuberance'. We started to listen to American and European news, the movements of indices like the Dow, Footsie, DAX, and the S&P 500 futures at the 24-hour Globex market, and of course FED-President Greenspan, just as every American trader did. That was the first step on the way to becoming international investors.

Riding the bull

In the end of 1996 I made money with two stocks: one of them was my darling, the oil company MOL, which had moved from the OTC market to the Exchange in early 1996. While almost all the other stocks surged to new highs, it stayed low for long. I thought that sooner or later it would surely follow the others, and when I saw my theory proved, I bought five thousand shares at prices ranging from 1700 to 2200 forints. The price skyrocketed, and after about a month I decided to sell at 3500 forints; I made the deal on my new mobile phone from a ski-slope in France (mobile phone systems had just been installed).

My other investment was the share of a chemical company, TVK. It came on the market in August at a low price. I bought 5000 shares, but it stayed there, almost unchanged, for months, while others doubled or tripled. Finally, it started to move up and I sold at about 30% higher than I had bought, but it was too early; within a month the price had doubled.

And we shouldn't forget the good old compensation note. In late 1995, it had fallen to as low as 14% of its face value. One of my brokers suggested buying immediately. I thought that at this price, so close to zero, it wasn't a big risk. Sooner or later, the government had to provide something for it. I bought 5000 notes at 14 and the price skyrocketed immediately! At 22 I added another 5000 notes and sold the whole package at 33. Though I made a profit of almost 100%,

Adventurous moneymaking

I could have done even more! The price surged further, all the way to 120 in one year, much higher then anytime in its history. And as I heard from other traders, note buying and selling was booming again, just as in 1992-94. I should have gotten in again. The young guy who led me to the 200-contract friend, organized it perfectly and made good money out of it.

What had caused such a fast rise? The government decided to offer the shares of the newly privatized regional electricity companies in exchange for notes. There were so many shares that almost all the outstanding notes could be used, and demand was high: their main owners (like German RWE) were buying these energy shares until they acquired 70% or more in these companies.

Then I had an ingenious idea. These electricity shares were not listed on the Stock Exchange yet, they were at the OTC market. I knew which brokerage company was buying the shares of a certain electricity company for RWE; a friend of mine worked there. They were calling other brokerage firms to ask if they had any stocks to sell. As the brokerage houses felt the selling pressure, they started to sell only at higher prices. I thought if there was only one buyer, the stocks could be collected without bigger increases in price. So I suggested to my friend that they should buy from me, and stop buying from the brokerage companies. I promised big quantities at a fixed price.

Now I was the only buyer on the market. I called the brokerage companies and told them that I would buy, but didn't urge them. As they saw that the other company (the big institution) stopped buying, they immediately called me (the only buyer) and dumped as many shares as I wanted. I collected the whole package RWE planned to buy in a month.

The Asian Contagion

In early 1997, the rally on emerging markets entered a bubble period. The ever-rising prices attracted both private and institutional investors. Numerous funds emerged specializing in Eastern Europe; money was pouring into these funds from all around the world. The smart money started to leave, the stupid to come. The market index surged 50% in just one month! That was my cue to sell my shares in MOL and TVK.

Then the market fell back sharply. As I expected a further surge in their prices, I decided to buy the same two stocks again when their prices had dropped about 20%. This time I was buying not only with cash, but on margin as well. At first it proved to be a good idea, as the whole market, including my stocks, started to surge again. But now in this last, overbought phase of the bull market, more and more people were buying, and more and more on margin.

This phase is dangerous for the market: any pullback could ignite a panic selling, a lot of margin calls, and at the end, liquidation. The liquidation of shares and futures positions pushes prices sharply lower and this way forces others to dump their shares when the margin call is coming.

Up until the summer, there were no signs of trouble. Prices rose higher every day. Everybody was optimistic – a bad sign! There were some days my stocks surged 5-10%. I was blinded, just like most investors. I should have taken the profit, seeing this mania on the market, but, unfortunately, I became greedy. The market was so oversubscribed that it would only take a spark to burst the bubble. And the spark soon arrived.

One hot summer day, prices started to fall sharply. The reason, as we realized later: economic crisis in some of the fast-developing countries of Southeast Asia. In the previous months, the smaller Asian currencies had become overvalued against the US dollar, until the point where they crashed. The first one was the baht, the currency of Thailand. Foreign capital started to leave the country and this ignited a domino effect: the same soon happened in Indonesia, Malaysia and Korea. Money started to flow out of other emerging markets, and after a time, the western stock markets were effected as well.

By the time I realized what the problem was, my stocks had already fallen a lot. I hoped it was only a correction. First everything seemed rosy again, but then in October, the stock market in Hong Kong crashed, and 3 days later, the Dow tumbled 500 points, the biggest daily point loss since 1987. The next day, almost all shares were suspended in Budapest, because of the 20% drop in the market. When trading resumed, they rose, but not strongly enough. The trouble wasn't over yet. In November, the stock markets calmed down a bit all over the world, even in Asia, but not in Budapest. That market fell even further. The reason: there were enormous positions bought on margin. The liquidation of these positions lasted 5 days and during this short period the market fell about 25%. On the last day, I sold all my shares bought on margin and kept the others. I wasn't forced; I simply didn't want to risk a loss after letting a huge paper profit melt down.

I think this was my first real shock during my time on the markets. Since then, I have seen this liquidation spiral many times, mainly on the Nasdaq. One should trigger a *profit lock-in*, especially if trading on margin. In my case, there had been enough time, several months, to decide where to say, 'I won't let it go lower.' But I was greedy and just waited and hoped...

After this shock, we decided to go to Thailand for a holiday with a friend. We had been suffering because of Asia for months; why not go there to enjoy it a bit? During the wonderful time we spent there, my remaining stocks started to rise, and continued rising until the end of the year. The Asian Contagion was over and markets rose again, especially in the US and Europe.

El Nino and Croesus

In January 1998, the rally continued. I sold my MOL and TVK shares when I had a nice profit on them; I didn't want to make the same mistake again. MOL rose further, up another 40% from the level where I had sold. This time I shouldn't have sold it because it rose healthily, with only small corrections. Earlier, when I hadn't sold it in time, there had been a huge and ugly distribution of the stock. If I had had a profit lock-in with, let's say 30% of the reached profit, I would have sold much earlier at a good price then, and I would have kept longer and sold at a much higher price now in early 1998.

At this point, I didn't have any idea about the market direction, so I left the stocks a bit. The compensation note seemed to promise a good opportunity instead. The state offered its remaining energy shares for notes. I thought they were worth buying; RWE and other big companies would be interested again. For about 3-4 weeks, I once again placed ads in the newspaper to buy compensation notes. The note holders were coming to my office, just like old times. I collected a nice package and exchanged it for energy shares. My expectation was correct: the price of these shares more than doubled in the next few months. I was sitting on these shares; they were rising, so there was nothing to do. My wife and I decided it was high time for a vacation. We planned to go to sunny Florida and the Caribbean. In Florida we were unlucky; it was cool and raining because of El Nino, but things were better in Jamaica, warm and sunny, as it should be.

When we returned, I noticed that one of my favorites, the chemical share TVK, was rising. It kept going up day by day. I decided to buy 5000 shares. It kept rising and rising, so I was quite satisfied. In just a few weeks I had turned a 30% profit; I sold half of my shares to secure a part of it. Two days later, a fund (with a good name: Croesus) announced that they had bought about 25% of the outstanding TVK shares! The price surged immediately after the news, but then started to slide. As the fund stopped buying, there were no more big buyers. I sold the other half of my package, at exactly the same price as the first half, but this time on the way down. The decision proved clever as the price fell even further.

4. THE RUSSIAN CRISIS

The new capitalist miracle

In 1998, the price of crude oil shrank to $10 a barrel. It was incredibly cheap in real terms, maybe cheaper than it had been before the first oil crisis in 1973. Of course it was good for the economy of most countries, but at the same time it was devastating for oil exporters, especially for Russia, where the economy was still not strong enough to cope several years after the collapse of communism. The Russian State had less and less income in hard currencies from oil exports; its currency reserves were decreasing. The Russian currency, the rouble, should have been devalued to cope with the situation, but it was pegged to the dollar. Instead of devaluation, the government decided to attract foreign currency to the country at any price. They issued treasuries with a yield of more than 100%. But that was a dangerous practice: how could they pay that enormous debt later?

Investors didn't care. They were blinded by the 100 percent yield – although they had seen what could happen in such a situation, just a year earlier in Asia. They said Russia was different. But why would it have been different? It was a country with less industry

The Russian crisis

than Southeast Asia, and almost its only source of income was oil and gas.

Prices on the Moscow Stock Exchange had been skyrocketing in the previous two years – investors had been waiting for some kind of 'economic miracle' after the fall of communism. A lot of foreign, first of all American, money had already been invested in Russia, and that summer, the money was pouring in – to its destiny. As Russia ran out of its currency reserves, default became inevitable.

At that time I was still operating mainly on the Hungarian market. We found it ironic how just ten years earlier we had kept an eye on Moscow to see whether we would be allowed more freedom, and now we kept an eye on its wild capitalist stock market to help predict our market direction.

As some listed companies on the Stock Exchange had huge markets in Russia, they were sensitive to any economic changes in the former communist behemoth. We had just noticed that these stocks started to fall. First of all the leader of the big bull market in the previous years, Richter Pharmaceutical; at least a third of its products were sold in Russia. It reached 25,000 forints ($120) earlier that year, but came down to 17,000 ($80) in early summer. There were huge offers: institutions were selling and a lot of individuals and small funds, who believed that it was a bargain after falling 30%, were buying. The price stayed there for weeks – a huge distribution. Then one day, after the crowd of investors had bought to the limit, there

Adventurous moneymaking

were no more bids and the price collapsed and plunged to 4000 forints ($21-22).

It was a valuable lesson, one that I had learned earlier: a share is not a bargain just because it has fallen 20, 30, or even 50% in a short period of time. Over the next two years I talked to a lot of people who were stuck in Richter. I asked them about the price at which they had bought and the answer was always at or a bit over 17,000 forints ($80). All of them bought when the smart institutions, maybe insiders among them, were selling at the same price for weeks.

Shares of some other companies dependent on the Russian market also suffered. However, one of them, Zalakeramia, a company exporting building materials to Russia and elsewhere, remained quite high. I sold it short at 7800 forints, and as I saw I was right when it fell further, I sold some more at 5800. It was a good idea: in a few weeks time I closed the shorts at about 2000 forints!

The crash

The Stock Exchange was still open only 3 hours a day. It meant that all the bids and offers had to be executed quickly; there was no time for waiting for corrections if prices moved sharply. Volatility was extremely high and panics occurred often. Trading with Hungarian shares continued in London on the SEAQ system after hours, so prices could move further there. As a result, the

Budapest market opened the next day with a huge gap; prices were often 10% or more different from the closing prices of the previous day (just as happens today on the Nasdaq or the NYSE, after an up- or downgrade). Most Hungarian investors couldn't trade on the London market so the risk was enormous; one had to expect huge shifts in the price of any stock at any time. But people didn't care. There had been a bull market for two and a half years and investors were buying what they considered bargains, even on margin, and they opened lots of contracts of long futures. The market became a hidden bomb that could explode anytime.

And then Russia defaulted. Nothing worse could have happened! First only the rouble was devalued, after having been kept artificially high for so long. Then suddenly investors understood the situation, but by then it was too late. They wanted to withdraw their money; everybody was trying to exit through the same door. It couldn't last long: Russia didn't have currency reserves any more, so it became insolvent. Every payment was halted. All those who had rushed to invest their money in a country believed to be the land of dreams, lost everything. Huge amounts of money were stuck in Russia.

On August 20 panic selling started on all the markets. The Dow, the Nasdaq, the Footsie, the DAX and all other indices tumbled, some of them by 4-5% a day. Emerging markets, like the Brazilian Bovespa, were losing 10% a day. But maybe the biggest loser, after Moscow of course, was the Budapest market. From

7500 points just before the crisis, the benchmark BUX index fell by half, to 3700 points, in just 3 weeks. One reason was simple: there were a lot of stocks to sell, and only 3 hours a day for trading. There was no time for any retreat. Another reason was that emerging market funds were full of Russian stocks and bonds, and they immediately sold any of their other stocks that could be sold in big quantities. The Hungarian market was quite liquid so they could sell enormous packets of stocks, and that of course pushed down prices sharply.

After the market started tumbling, I sold Richter short at 11.000 forints (about $55). In three days it was below 7000 ($35). What a trade! I took the big profit, only to watch it fall even further. Nothing could stop the free-fall.

As the market continued its crash, I placed index futures bids at very low prices every day in the opening session, in which the price was calculated by a special allocation. I thought if there was a big panic before the opening, I could catch some bargains and sell them later, when the market had calmed down a bit during the day. On one of these panic days I saw that the BUX index futures opened at 4000 points instead of the 5000 that would have been justified by the prompt market. I got my 40 contracts. We couldn't understand where such a gift was coming from...

In a few minutes, we knew the answer. A big brokerage firm had liquidated all its positions and placed the offers at 1 point, the lowest possible price. Surely it would have been enough to place their offer about

20% under the previous day's price to sell all their contracts. In five minutes, the price got back to normal levels. For me, it meant a $20,000 present!

Worldwide turmoil

Why was the selling so heavy worldwide? The answer is simple: there simply wasn't enough money available. Russia swallowed more than 100 billion dollars, and this sum was so huge that liquidity decreased sharply on all markets. Funds needed immediate cash to replace what they lost in Russia, so they had to dump shares with no price limit. That forced the liquidation of other long positions, and that pushed stock prices even lower. Some hedge funds ran out of cash. One of the biggest, LTCM (Long-Term Capital Management) went bankrupt. A liquidity crisis, a credit crunch was arising.

Markets fell heavily further, and on the last day of August, the Dow tumbled 500 points once again, just like ten months earlier. The next day it opened even lower, but in half an hour it turned and a huge rally started. The FED acted by immediately covering some of the losses arising from the bankruptcy of LTCM and thus providing some liquidity. However, the rally lasted only that day, and then markets were tumbling again. Incredible panic spread around the world. Financial stocks led the free-fall, as these were most sensitive to the financial crisis: JP Morgan fell from $50 to $25.

I could see no improvement on the horizon and as I expected further falling, I shorted again. This was an enormous mistake, with the market so oversold. The Budapest Stock Exchange had performed especially badly; the benchmark index had fallen from over 8000 points down to 3700 points. But some blue chips still seemed relatively high, among them MTelekom, which was listed on the NYSE as well. I shorted it, and waited for a fall of another 30%.

At the beginning of October, the markets fell once again, as I expected, but this time prices couldn't hit new lows. The Dow made a double bottom at 7500 points, 20% from its previous top. In some opinions, if the decline is less than 20% from the previous high, that is still considered a bull market, if the price falls more than 20% from the top, it's the start of a bear market. Since then, we've heard a lot about this barrier of bulls and bears. The final defeat of the bull was in 2001, when the S&P 500 and the Dow were flirting with the 20% level for months before they broke it.

But then, still in October 1998, the bull market remained intact, in spite of the turmoil caused by the Russian crisis. The Dow started to climb from 7500 points, and it was the first time I looked at the Nasdaq Composite. It was around 1350 points; it still wasn't attracting much attention...

Despite my expectations, my MTelekom didn't seem to want to fall any further. It started climbing – I should have realized that it's a bad sign for the bears and closed the shorts immediately. Instead, I started to hope that it would go the right way. Hope, this very human thing, can be one of the biggest enemies of the trader, alongside fear and greed. The stock trader often hopes when he should fear, and fears when he should hope. I should have feared that my stock sold short would go higher, and my loss increase. Instead, I hoped that it would fall, maybe the very next day. A trader must fear of the increasing loss, and hope when the position is performing, hope that it goes further the right way, and the profit will increase.

My broker said that an older colleague who had traded a lot in different markets, said: 'Sell your house and car, and buy shares! This is a rare occasion.' At the same time, Andre Kostolany said: 'Buy Russian shares, only Russian.' They were both right. They had the experience of a lifetime. Markets recovered, and especially Russian shares. Some of them are now 100-fold what they were in the worst days of the crisis.

Greenspan saves the world

So a rally started in October, and then Greenspan, the momentum player, made a big, half percentage point rate-cut. It gave a boost to the markets; they started skyrocketing. It became obvious that the FED could handle the liquidity crisis, and thus save the world economy. This was followed by two other big rate cuts in the next two months. And then crude oil started to rise: there was light at the end of the Russian tunnel.

It was obvious that a market as deeply oversold as the Hungarian one must skyrocket. I knew that I should own as many stocks as possible, but instead of this I was short, and my loss became so enormous that I would have had hardly any money left if I closed the shorts. The reader may wonder how this was possible: the brokerage firm should have closed it out when the margin was not sufficient. But this was a small brokerage company without strict rules and my position was not so big as to be dangerous for them, so they let me keep the position open as long as I had even one penny left in my account.

On the Stock Exchange, everybody knew that I had short positions. Only a few of us were bearish; of course the majority were bullish, all the way down! As long as the market was tumbling, they envied and admired us, bears. We were even humming in the visitors' gallery! But once the market turned, I didn't dare enter the visitors' gallery. The pain of the losing positions was bad enough; I didn't want to see the victorious and malicious faces of the bulls too. I returned to my office and started thinking about what to do.

After a day or two, I had a brilliant idea: I knew that when I sold short, the selling price of the stocks got to my account (impossible in any market today, but that was a young emerging market). I thought that bellwethers like MTelekom would rise first, and in the next phase, smaller stocks could join the rally, and rise much faster than blue chips. So I remained short of MTelekom, and from the price of it I bought

Zalakeramia and other small-caps, as well as some index futures. Then I went to Austria on vacation. I was sure I was right and I didn't want to see what was happening on the market every day!

The idea worked; MTelekom only rose another 10%, while at the same time Zalakeramia skyrocketed 70%. This spread saved me, and my long futures performed beautifully as well.

After a while, I called my broker from Austria. He told me the prices; they seemed incredible! The BUX index had risen 30%, and my long futures had made me more than $100,000! I told my broker to close them immediately. Such a big profit, in such a short period of time, it must be taken anyway I thought. As I arrived home, I was surprised to learn that I had sold at the top, a rare occasion in a trader's life.

About a week later, I traveled to Canada, where my wife had eye surgery. From there I called my broker again; prices were much lower than a week earlier. I decided to open 200 contracts again. Then, sitting on the longs and waiting for the new rally, we flew from Toronto to Puerto Rico for a long weekend which made up for the cold and rain in Florida the previous winter.

By this time, all the big markets had risen a lot since hitting bottom just six weeks earlier. The Nasdaq surged to 2000 points again (up 50%), and the Dow rose from 7500 to 9000 points. Just like in the panic earlier, financial institutions were also the leaders in the rally: JP Morgan rose to $60, higher than the pre-crisis price.

Thanksgiving and the Web

The next weekend was Thanksgiving. American markets were closed; other markets simply didn't know what to do. They had followed America in the previous weeks; now there was nothing to follow. My long positions were performing wonderfully and I should have taken the profit. But I was stubborn; I expected the Hungarian market to return to its pre-crisis level, just like the American markets had done. I didn't take into consideration the fact that European markets didn't reach these levels. The effects of the default of Russia were more serious in Europe.

After Thanksgiving, US markets fell sharply. Maybe the long weekend gave investors a little time to think, and maybe they decided to take the huge profits of the previous weeks. Maybe others just wanted to get out of the stocks they had been stuck in during the terrible weeks of the Russian turmoil. In any case, they dumped their shares for a few days.

After the first day of tumbling on Wall Street, the BUX index opened with a huge gap down. I closed out the 200 long contracts with a mild loss. Had I closed 5 days earlier, before Thanksgiving, I would have had a nice profit, about $50,000!

Since then, I stop trading before Thanksgiving. The market is even less predictable than at other times of the year. I can't really explain the cause. Maybe funds rebalance their portfolios, or investors decide to sell to have cash before Christmas, while others rush to buy because they expect a Santa Claus rally. Price movements become wild, especially on the first trading days after the long weekend.

So after the Thanksgiving dip still in 1998, markets rose slowly in December. The Russian crisis was over, and many stocks and indices were as high as before the crisis. Investors decided then that whatever crisis and turmoil might come in the world, these are good buying opportunities because it was a bull market. And they were right, for another year. The wildest period of the big bull was still to come.

I began to pay more and more attention to different markets all around the world. Until then it had been difficult because only investors who subscribed to Reuters or other systems could see the markets and these were very expensive; few people could afford it. But then a new and wonderful thing appeared and completely changed traders' life: it was the Internet, the World Wide Web. Suddenly it became easy to study any market, to follow prices, and to read news and comments. I think this was really a revolutionary step for investors. Until that time, trading on different markets of the world, or on US markets from outside America was really difficult. Now it became a reality.

In the mornings, I went online in the office, and surfed on the Web. Then I went to the Stock Exchange, to the journalists' room. There we traded, collected materials for articles, discussed the market, and had enough time for telling stories and joking besides. Just like Andre Kostolany had done a few decades earlier in his favorite city, Paris. There were many visitors and traders in the visitors' gallery, which was next to the journalists' room. About a hundred people were there each day, and the atmosphere was a very good indicator of the market.

In the afternoons, after the market close, I went back to the office, just next door to the Stock Exchange. I wrote articles and sent them by e-mail to the newspaper, while following the American markets, which just opened when European markets closed. I even had some chat room windows open.

But these were the last months of the Budapest Stock Exchange as a trading floor, as a gathering place for traders, journalists and visitors. Full scale computerized trading replaced the open outcry and the brokers left the floor; they could trade in their offices, just like on the Nasdaq, the London Stock Exchange or the Xetra in Frankfurt. There was a celebration to say goodbye to the floor and the building itself. We were allowed to enter the empty trading floor and we could even ring the closing bell, the very last time.

Then in the spring of 1999, Andre Kostolany died. He had wanted to live at least until the first days of the year 2000. He knew, with his experience of decades, that even he would be able to see something new on the markets then. Unfortunately he couldn't be with us in those exciting days. We miss his stories and comments, and we always will. We say so many times even today: I wonder what Kosto would say in this or that situation...

Bulgarian adventure

One of my new friends from the Stock Exchange was a young economist. His father was Bulgarian, so he spent a lot of time in Bulgaria. One day, he mentioned that the Stock Exchange was just opening there; stocks were still fundamentally very cheap. He suggested that we go and look around. With other guys, among them some brokerage company owners, we traveled to the Bulgarian capital, Sofia. There we went to a bank where my friend had some connections, and opened accounts. We studied the shares and the general situation and found that the market was still not liquid; there would have been buyers for the cheap stocks but there were no offers, so we placed our bids and left.

A few weeks later, when we saw that we couldn't buy anything, we decided to buy the stocks aggressively at whatever prices we could, among them the former state oil monopoly Neftochim, some companies owning hotels on the shore of the Black Sea (Albena and Golden Sands), tobacco companies (Blagoevgrad, Bulgartabak Holding), and others. After a time, we got the shares. At first everything was all right. But later, the crisis of the big Slavic brother ruined the young Bulgarian market. We sold our shares with a huge loss.

My friend wouldn't give up. He suggested setting up a small fund investing in Bulgaria, to buy the even cheaper stocks. We agreed and the fund exists still today, making a solid growth each year. I wish our fund had invested in Russia, where prices had risen 100-fold since then...

Adventurous moneymaking

In between, a really interesting situation occured. My friend had another Bulgarian friend, who studied economy first in Budapest, later in Boston in the US. Back in 1997, we had spent a few days with him in Boston. A year later, he started to work for a brokerage company in London. There he met the son of the former Bulgarian king, and when the 2002 elections were approaching in Bulgaria, they formed a political party. They traveled to Sofia, built their party, and won the elections. The former king became the Prime Minister, and our friend the deputy Prime Minister.

I am optimistic about their leadership and their task of making Bulgaria a prospering capitalist country ready to join the EU. They accelerated the privatization process (which was more or less over everywhere else in Eastern Europe by this time). Western investors appeared on the stock market, prices started rising, and our little fund started performing quite well. Our best investment was Blagoevgrad, one of the local tobacco companies: it rose 500% within 2 years. Compensation notes have been introduced in Bulgaria too; available at a low price (24% of face value) for long. An enormous speculation opportunity, as we will see!

5. THE BUBBLE

Brazil crisis

The last year in the old millennia, 1999, started with an enormous 3-day rally. All indices rose sharply, but one seemed even stronger than the others, and that was the Nasdaq. It had been at 1350 points in the Russian crisis and now it was over 2000 points, a gain of well over 50% in a 3-month period. It was the beginning of the tech-bubble.

On January 1, the new common European currency, the euro, was launched. At this stage the euro only existed in accounts; national currencies continued to circulate as banknotes and coins for another 3 years. On the stock markets, prices were quoted in euro from this time.

About a week later the markets became nervous once again. This time Brazil was in economic crisis, and its currency had to be devalued. It had been pegged to the dollar and became extremely overvalued; the country ran out of dollars just like Russia had a few months earlier. However, this time the effect on the markets wasn't so strong. This case was less dangerous because there wasn't so much hot money in Brazil: investors had taken it out in time, still during and after their adventure in Russia. Markets fell for a few days, but it was nothing more than a correction. The bull was strong: investors considered the Brazil crisis as an excellent buying opportunity.

The question arises: Why are there so many crises in developing countries? And why do they have such an effect on the world economy and on markets?

The reason is the same in each case. These countries peg their currencies to the US dollar or other strong currencies. But at the same time, they don't have a rigorous fiscal and monetary policy, which would be essential to keep their currency as strong as the US dollar. They start building up a deficit, and then print money to cover it. This huge flood of money fuels inflation, and the goods produced in the country become more expensive in local currency. Those who produce goods for export, mainly for US and European markets, get the same amount in their currency when they change their dollars (or euros), while their costs (labor, raw material, energy etc) are rising. After a time, selling the goods abroad is not a business anymore, so exports start to decline. At the same time, the price of imported goods doesn't rise, so they become relatively cheaper than those produced locally.

With exports declining and imports increasing, the country spends more and more dollars or other major currencies on imports and gets less and less for its exports. Currency reserves shrink, and one day the country run out of currency reserves. That is the crisis. The country suspends all payments abroad, and of course cannot import goods any more. In the end it is forced to devalue its currency, but then devaluation means 100% or more, so the buying power and the living standard of the country falls to a fraction of what it was.

In this way, huge markets for mainly American and European goods disappear from one day to another. It hurts American and European economies, and especially certain companies, that were heavily exposed on that particular market.

This happened in 1995 in Mexico, 2 years later in Thailand, Malaysia, Indonesia, South Korea and Hong Kong, in 1998 in Russia, in 1999 in Brazil, and later in Turkey and Argentina. In most cases, the IMF and lending governments have to rescue these countries, avoiding their total collapse; they often have to pay tens of billions of dollars.

How could these crises be avoided? These countries should let their currencies float. In case of inflation, the market could devalue the currency gradually, thus keeping the balance of exports and imports in harmony. If the country wants a stable currency, it should control inflation with strict fiscal policy.

Dow 10,000!

After the crisis in Brazil, the rally continued on world markets. The Dow reached its earlier highs over 9000 points, and stayed there for a while. In April, it started to climb further, and soon got close to the 5-digit mark. There naturally appeared a lot of profit takers, thinking that maybe it could not exceed the magic number. Some institutions used sell-programs: whenever a price or an index approaches or reaches a resistance level, their computerized sell-program kicks in, and automatically starts selling shares from their portfolios. The buyers get a lot of shares, so the price can decline from the resistance level. But if the buyers are strong enough, they can sweep away the sell-programs, and the price breaks out. Then buy-programs come in at the former resistance level that now behaves as a support.

This happened to the Dow. After a few pullbacks, it got over 10,000 points, and after the breakout it rose further and stabilized well over 10,000. Investors and analysts became enthusiastic: some even started to guess how long it would take to get 100,000! These expectations could signal that the bull market might be soon over.

The Dow Jones had already risen a lot in a historically short period of time. It was still at 4000 in 1995, only four years earlier. It was just under 6000 at the time of Greenspan's 'irrational exuberance' speech. And we shouldn't forget that the Dow consists of blue chips, and these are usually not as volatile as some small-caps or tech stocks.

Let's look at how the Dow had performed earlier. It reached 1000 points in 1965 for the first time. But it was only in 1982 when it finally left this milestone

The bubble

behind for good. In between, there were smaller bull and bear markets and the Dow hovered between 500 and 1000 points; it took 17 years to get over the four-digit mark!

What if it takes the same amount of time to leave 10,000 finally behind? It would be absolutely normal, if we examine the long-term chart:

FIGURE 1

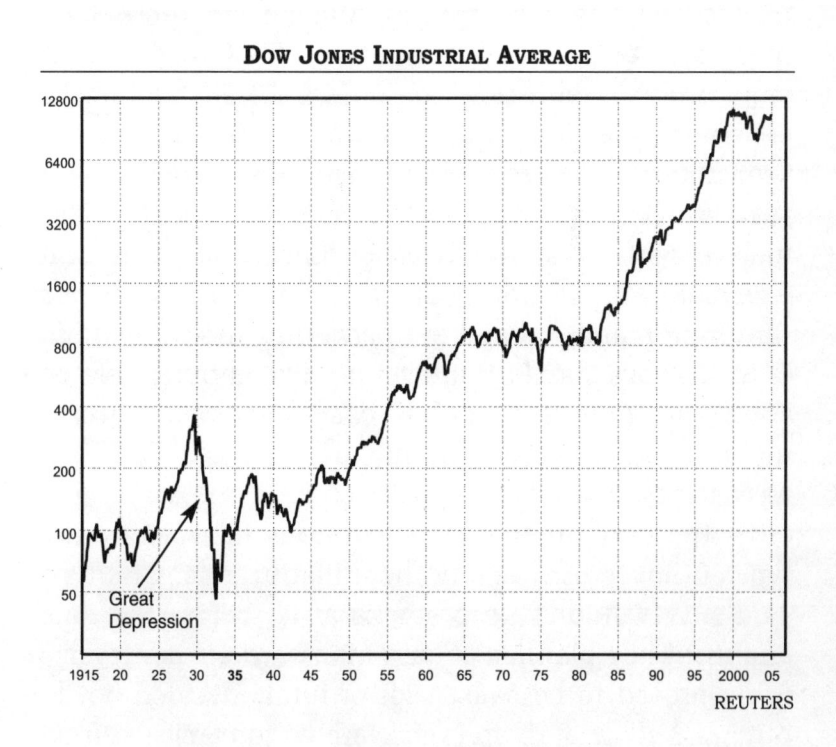

DOW JONES INDUSTRIAL AVERAGE

REUTERS

Meanwhile, other markets and indices were rising as well. The fastest was the Nasdaq, which reached 2500 points, almost twice its bottom in the Russian crisis. The S&P 500 was at 1300 points, 10% higher than before and 30% higher than during the crisis. In Europe, the DAX was at 5500 points, while the Footsie reached its pre-crisis top, 6000 points.

Y2K-bug

In the last years before the Millennium there were more and more worries about the 'Y2K-bug', a possible problem with how computers would handle the change in the first two digits when 1999 became the year 2000. It seemed a bit strange that this could be a real problem: computer programmers have to solve more serious tasks hundreds of times a day. I think it was mainly a psychological effect, but it was so strong that fund managers and even governments were afraid of it. Rumors spread that everything computer-related could break down, first of all cash machines. Governments decided to print enormous amounts of cash just in case.

In the run up to the Millennium there were two types of investors, among them institutions. One type said they wouldn't keep stocks at all before the date change. They planned to buy afterwards, when everything proved to be safe. A lot of funds decided not to buy, and some of them even planned to be closed from November 1999 until mid January 2000. The other type, and I think the bigger group, thought that they

The bubble

should buy before the big day, while prices were still low. They thought, absolutely logically, that Y2K might not be a serious problem for mankind.

All of us who wanted to buy before 'D-day', January 1, waited for a panic selling. A big sell-off was under way in September and October, as we expected. But, on a certain day, on October 18, the market turned and started rising. From that moment, it never looked back until the big day.

In the next two and a half months, we saw the biggest ever skyrocketing in such a short period, on stock markets all around the world. It seemed unbelievable. I of course didn't believe it, and made the same mistake I'd made a year earlier: I sold short against the trend. I thought the market must fall, but for some reason it couldn't. We didn't understand why but there was a huge rally. Finally I'd learnt my lesson: don't fight the trend, even if it goes against what seems logical!

In the first days of December the rally accelerated to an incredible level. A trader in London called us to ask, 'Who do you think is buying so vehemently? All the big financial institutions like us are virtually closed in December and early January.' His question remained unanswered still for a few months.

Everybody could see that this was a big bull market even before the Millennium. All those who had short positions had to close them, and all those who planned to buy in the last part of the year now wanted to jump on the bandwagon. I of course closed my shorts, and just in time too.

Meanwhile, the Nasdaq reached and passed 3000 points. Tech stocks went through the roof. I thought the investors would have to pay a heavy price for this mania sooner or later. The Nasdaq more than doubled in one year, not even stopping for a sound correction. It seemed like an easy get-rich-quick scheme: just buy any stock at any time and wait a few days or weeks until it doubles. In December 1999 it really was: on the last day of the year the Nasdaq Composite printed at 4000 points.

Some stocks reached their top (Microsoft at $60, Lucent at $80, Qualcomm at $180, Yahoo at $250!), earlier than most shares. Others were still on their way up, but already at unbelievable highs (Verisign at $200, Broadcom at $130). The British Footsie reached its peak then at 7000 points, while the German DAX soared 30% in the last two months of the year!

At the last minute I changed my position, closing the shorts and opening long index futures and buying some individual shares. I thought that there could be nothing else after the Big Day, just an even more giant rally, no matter how big it already had been before it. To tell the truth, I expected a rally on the emerging markets, especially in Central Europe, for the whole year 2000. I considered them relatively cheap with a P/E ratio of about 10-12, while other markets were much more expensive fundamentally. I still believed the 'convergence story', which said that the stock markets of Central and Eastern European countries, especially the EU applicants, would rise as long as there was such a gap between the valuations of stocks on these markets and the developed markets of Europe. There had been a huge rally in Greece, which was a relatively new EU member, and this fact fed our hopes.

We spent the last days of the old millennia and New Year's Eve in sunny Athens. I watched TV from the early afternoon on New Year's Eve: the first time zones in the Pacific and New Zealand had just stepped into 2000, and a few hours later Southeast Asia and then Russia followed. As I expected, everything was all right around the world. I hoped markets could do nothing but cheer the happy new millennia, and my shares and futures would bring a huge profit. My wife and I left CNN and went to the Acropolis to see the fireworks.

Fait accompli

The first trading day of the new year was just as expected: all the markets went to the sky. The Dow rose over 11,000, the Nasdaq over 4000, the DAX to 8000 points (after being below 4000 during the Russian crisis). But then, on the next day, buyers got exhausted and the markets started to decline, to my surprise. It was a case of *fait accompli*: the good news was there, but the majority had bought for it in advance; there wasn't enough buying power left for a further big rally. My small emerging market, the Budapest Stock Exchange, was closed for two more days. By the time it opened, world markets were already lower than on the last trading day of 1999; I didn't have time for profit taking. After three days of relentless decline, I decided to close my futures, still turning a small profit. I didn't understand what was going on so at this point I got out of the market.

That was a huge disappointment. I should have been suspicious after that giant rally in 1999; I should have realized it wouldn't be so easy. Those who had bought that enormous quantity of stocks had to sell sooner or later. But why did they buy then, and why sell immediately now?

The explanation came only in February. The FED, fearing the possible outcome of Y2K, had started not only to print enormous quantities of banknotes, but also sharply increased the money supply of banks from as early as the middle of October. Then, seeing that everything was all right after January 1, it withdrew this supply until the middle of February.

That was the source of the money that had fed the endless rally for more than two months in the old year, and as it was withdrawn, the same money left the market in January, causing sharp fallbacks in stock prices. At the same time, all those funds that had waited to buy until after the turning of the year now made a heavy demand so sharp rallies and declines followed each other in the first weeks of the year.

The situation was the same on emerging markets too. Sharp rallies and declines followed each other at no more than three-day intervals. Sometimes I bought stocks or opened long futures but jumped out soon because of these sudden, unpredictable movements. I still expected the emerging markets to be bullish for the year. I hoped that sooner or later the market would calm down a bit so I could buy again.

There was one thing I didn't pay enough attention to. From early 1999, the FED had raised interest rates several times throughout the year. The ECB, the European Central Bank and the Bank of England followed its lead. Now that there were the two giant currencies, the US dollar and the euro, and the smaller but still important British pound between them, these three central banks acted more or less together.

Rate hikes sooner or later do harm for the stock market, especially when it has been rising for so long. There's less money to feed the market, and when that is the case, funds start leaving the riskier emerging markets first. The giant and atypical money supply of Greenspan from October to December turned everything upside down, generating a huge rally, but now in the year 2000 the effect of the rate hikes became stronger, and money quietly started to leave these fragile markets.

Final tech bubble

From the end of January, the Dow and everything else not related to technology started to fall heavily. Stocks were lumped into two groups: new economy and old economy. Everybody was trying to get rid of old economy stocks and buy new economy ones, no matter how expensive they were.

That was the final phase of the tech bubble. Stock exchanges all over the world opened new sections for tech stocks: Neuer Markt, Nuovo Mercato, Nouveau Marche; it was the same silly name 'New Market' in each language, and the same old story: technology makes endless profit, share prices can only go up and up. And the public believed this, although everybody should know that in the capitalist system there is no endless profit in the long term. If there is a big profit, then other companies immediately jump in, competition takes over and the profit falls back to normal levels.

It was the same when rail was new 200 years ago, and later it happened with oil; in the 1920s it was the radio and car industry, in the 1970s, computers. They were all new; the public believed the endless-growth story and created a bubble, which at last had to burst. The new markets disappeared. The best companies of the new industries continued to grow and perform well, while other companies went bankrupt, just like in other industries. A generation learnt the lesson. But then, after 30 years or so, when new industries emerge, everything starts again.

However, this time the bubble was bigger than at any other time in history, with stocks reaching valuations like never before and more people than ever jumping on the bandwagon. Many of them started to spend profits that hadn't been realized yet; they did not sell

The bubble

the shares but spent the money as if they had. When stock prices declined, the profit disappeared and only a huge debt remained.

The bubble reached its biggest size in early March; the Nasdaq peaked at over 5000 points, with prices such as Cisco at $80, QLogic at $200, Broadcom at $250, PMC-Sierra at $220, and Verisign at $260. In Europe, Deutsche Telekom reached €100, Infineon €70, SAP €270, France Telecom €220 and British mania-stock Baltimore Technologies an amazing £150 (three years later it was at 18 *pence* a share, one-thousandth of its peak price).

These stocks and other techs started to fall sharply after the peak on March 11. QLogic tumbled from 200 to 50, Broadcom from 250 to 110, PMC-Sierra from 220 to 120, and Verisign from 260 to 90 dollars! In 2 months, the Nasdaq Composite lost one third of its peak value, falling to 3300 from 5000 points.

But the bubble didn't burst immediately; it was so big that it took still a long time. During this period, many investors started to buy what they believed to be the dips. They thought these were just pullbacks, excellent buying opportunities. Smart investors dumped their shares; others just bought what they considered bargains, with P/E ratios of 100 or more.

The situation was the same not only on other big markets, but on emerging markets as well. On the Budapest Stock Exchange, mainly American funds started to buy telecom shares and some others that were seen as tech and Internet shares. When one of them, a retailer (my third share ten years earlier, Fotex), started to sell goods online, the price skyrocketed, just because investors considered it a dot-com company. These shares soared and reached their peak at the same time as the tech shares on the Nasdaq, and lost their values just like those. Unfortunately I missed shorting them.

By this time it had become obvious that the emerging market rally, and every kind of bull market, was over. I was watching the big markets carefully, first and foremost the European and American ones. I decided to trade on these, but first I wanted to study their behavior and movements. And this was quite an interesting period, as a descending market emerged, with big relief rallies.

The first such big 'bear market rally' started in the summer: bargain hunters flooded the market, pushing the Nasdaq back above 4000 points. Many bubble stocks reached $150-200 dollars again (Verisign was selling at $200, and Broadcom at $270), and there were some which reached their peak only now, among them networking stocks Juniper ($240) and Ciena ($150). The broader marked peaked a bit later and slower then the techs. The S&P 500 got over 1500 points and stayed there a few months before it started to decline. In the first months after the tech-peak, investors switched to old economy stocks, so these fell more slowly.

Later, in the autumn, the decline accelerated. When everyone had bought the 'bargains', there were no more buyers and the tech-market crashed again. The Nasdaq fell below 3000 points, with Broadcom and Verisign under $100 again, and Yahoo at $30 (one-eighth of its peak!). What trading opportunities: shorting them over $200, and make a quick profit of more than 100 dollars a share!

There was a market bottom on October 18, on exactly the same day as a year earlier. A relief rally was coming as Greenspan fuelled hopes of a possible rate cut, but it wasn't strong enough. By the end of December, the S&P 500 had fallen to 1400 points. This was only 10% from its peak, still not a serious decline. The Nasdaq seemed much worse: it stood at 2500 points in the last days of the year 2000, half of its peak just 10 months earlier. And the bubble had just begun to burst.

Disaster

Emerging markets tumbled a long way over the course of the year. The Budapest Stock Exchange fell back to the same level as it had been in October '99. A year earlier, I wouldn't have believed this was possible.

One more terrible thing happened to me that made this year even more disastrous. In March, considering it cheap, I bought a lot of shares of Zalakeramia (the one I had traded so brilliantly in the Russian crisis). The company had a big debt, so the share price was as low as it had been during the Russian Crisis. Rumors started to circulate that this debt would be converted to one with a much lower interest rate (debt swap).

Adventurous moneymaking

There was heavy demand for the stock on the market, so I added more to my original package. After a few days, there were no more buying pressure, and the market just waited for the news about the debt swap. When it didn't come, the price started to ease, slowly at first. A good friend of mine who knew somebody in the management of the company assured me that the debt swap was imminent, that we only had to wait two more days. I just waited and hoped. What a mistake! If the price is going the wrong way, you have to take a stop-loss, no matter what anybody says!

The two days passed without any news of the swap. Meanwhile the price kept falling further, and my friend kept telling me to wait patiently. And then more bad news: one of the brokerage companies where I had my money was temporarily suspended. Nobody could take money out of it, at least for a while. My stock fell further, to a level at which my margin wasn't enough. I should have paid but I couldn't, because the money was stuck.

I was forced out of the shares, right at the bottom. Later the debt swap was done and the share rose, not as much as I had expected earlier, but it would have been enough to get out of it without a loss. Now I stood there, almost bankrupt. Both Kostolany and Livermore describe this situation.

Kostolany says a trader is not a real trader if he hasn't gone bankrupt at least two times in his life. He says that on some occasions he had been in situations so hopeless that he has considered suicide. Unfortunately he doesn't say anything about how he got out of these situations.

Livermore on the other hand explains every detail of his bankruptcies and how he became rich again. Before the First World War, he had to wait five long years, sitting heavily in debt, until the dull, sideways market became tradable again. Then he was able to exploit the bull market during the first half of the War, when the US still hadn't joined the war but was delivering weapons and other products to its allies.

6. 2001 – A BEAR ODYSSEY

My Finnish 'darling'

In the first days of 2001 the markets tumbled even further; the Nasdaq fell to 2250 points. Then the FED cut rates for the first time since the Russian crisis. The market cheered Greenspan: the Nasdaq this time surged 14% in one day! For me it was obvious that such a move in one day could only be a bear market rally. But did it matter? As long as there are big moves, crashes and rallies, I can trade them, I thought.

After this huge rally, stocks eased again. In the next two months, there were two more half-percentage point rate cuts, but it didn't help in the short term. All indices went to new lows, the S&P 500 fell more than 20% from the top, confirming the bear market. After the third rate cut, there were two days in one week when the Dow tumbled more than 300 points. The Nasdaq fell below 2000 points, this way the value of the tech laden index was less than 40% of its peak just one year before! It was the biggest panic in one week I had seen on the markets since the Russian crisis.

During the fast rally following this panic, I carefully watched what happened to different stocks. I found one which performed very well, the Finnish mobile phone giant Nokia. The share fell to €22.50 in the panic, but jumped to €29 during the next three days. I analyzed the company; compared to other techs, it didn't seem overvalued. Mobile phone sales were still rising around the world and Nokia's share in global sales was growing steadily. Its earning was 80 cents a share; it meant a P/E of 25-30, which was much lower than for most tech stocks that time. Therefore I decided that if the price came down to its previous low (€22-23) I would buy and hope for a fast rally.

The share is listed in Helsinki, Frankfurt and New York as well, thus it is trading 13 hours a day altogether and it is quite liquid on all markets. Although it is a European stock, the American market is as important for it as the European, if not more so.

I found another reason to buy Nokia. There were rumors of a profit warning from the company. Based on my analysis of how the stock had been performing, I couldn't imagine one, but even more importantly, I knew from past experience that if investors expect bad news, they sell their stocks and even sell short. When bad news is anticipated, there are no more sellers but rather buyers who want to cover their shorts. In such cases the price rises, sometimes sharply, after the warning.

That was what I expected in this case. I waited until early March when it reached my target price of €22.50 and bought 5000 shares. The market was still falling, but Nokia didn't get lower. On the contrary: the next day the price started to rise. It climbed slowly up to

€23.50, and then suddenly jumped to €26 with a gap when Nokia CEO Jorma Ollila denied the warning, saying he expected solid growth for the year. The next day I sold my shares, at just over €27. I could have waited a bit more: after such a gap, there's often a second wave up, especially when the share had been so oversold. In a few days it shot up to €30, without me. But of course I was still glad; the 15% profit on my first big package of Nokia shares was a huge step forward on the way of emerging from bankruptcy.

Then the markets started tumbling again, this time even faster than anytime in the previous 12 months. The S&P 500 fell to 1100 points, the Dow fell below 9000, and the Nasdaq as low as 1620, a third of its peak! Even the rate cuts didn't help much. Too many investors, still stuck in their expensive stocks, hoped that the rate cuts would help to turn the market, but of course it couldn't turn until they sold their stocks. As Kostolany says; first the stocks must flow from the weak hands to the strong ones.

The last phase of this fall was relentless, without correction. Each day another company issued a profit warning, or a brokerage house cut its rating on a stock. There was huge pessimism; the market was extremely oversold. I thought a big bear market rally was imminent. Nokia seemed relatively strong: it couldn't reach its former low of €22.50. I didn't buy it; I was waiting for the triple bottom. Maybe too many of us were waiting for the same thing and started buying earlier, so the stock simply couldn't go down that low.

The Easter rally

On April 3, there was a last panic day in Europe. The German DAX and the Footsie in London tumbled more than 3% in the first two trading hours, but then sellers stopped dumping and the market turned suddenly. An hour earlier it had been raining cats and dogs, now the sun was shining! That's the way of a bottom after such a huge sell-off.

An enormous rally had begun, but US stocks were still flat that day. They were waiting for a sign. It soon arrived: after the market close, Dell gave its forecast for the next quarter, predicting better than expected earnings. The S&P 500 and Nasdaq futures on the 24-hour Globex market went straight up to the sky, still after hours, and the next day brought an unbelievable rally on all markets. The Dow surged 400 points! I didn't dare buy; I thought the rally was too fast and furious. It wasn't. After such a relentless fall, when the market is so oversold, this is a normal reaction, and when it happens, it lasts more than just one day.

The next morning, a bad figure was released; I don't remember if it was unemployment, GDP or inflation. The important thing was that the market fell that day, but only gave back less than half of its gains from the previous day. It was a good sign. After the market close, there was a comment on CNN, referring to the rally of the previous day as a 'suckers' rally'. At that moment I knew that an even bigger rally was coming. If they consider a suckers' rally, the public and some funds open short positions or postpone their buying. The smart investors buy, and the real suckers sell short this time, so when the rally is coming, they are squeezed out of their shorts and that sparks an even bigger rally. That is exactly what happened this April.

The next day after this comment I was thinking about what to buy in Europe, still before the markets opened in the US. Most shares, including Nokia, were sharply higher. I found one American stock that wasn't higher in Europe than its previous closing price on the NYSE. It was AMD, the second US processor making company after Intel. It had plunged from 30 to less than 20 dollars in a few trading days; I thought if the market was bottoming, it wasn't a big risk, so I bought it in Frankfurt for about €22 (or $20 at that time).

On US markets, there was of course a big rally that day, but AMD and some other semiconductor stocks remained flat. I was impatient; I sold my shares with a profit of a few cents. Two hours later, all semiconductors joined the rally. AMD closed at $22, and in a few days it shot up to $30...

Now the earnings season was coming. The market was still oversold, there were lots of short positions, and the bears hoped that bad earnings could make prices fall again. Yes, earnings were poor. But instead of falling, stocks rose sharply again. The shorts were waiting for sellers in vain, then became impatient and closed their positions quickly. The fastest rallies can be ignited by short covering! When traders in short positions are squeezed, price doesn't matter any more;

they must buy immediately. That's why oversold rallies are fast and furious: they are a good opportunity for a quick profit.

In mid-April, the rally continued, becoming a real Easter rally. And now, when stock prices rose sharply, Greenspan took the momentum and cut rates for the fourth time. I tried to catch the momentum and bought Nokia immediately as it was passing its previous high, €31. I should have bought another stock, maybe an American one, or at least not only Nokia. It had already surged a lot in Europe, and after the rate cut, of course American shares started the big rally.

The next day Nokia released its earnings. The earnings were as expected; the price fell back a bit. I sold it with a small profit – once again too early. After some good figures, a new phase of the rally came in the last days of April and Nokia reached €38.

The Easter rally continued for five weeks, during which time I thought I had found a share that was still cheap. It was Yahoo, and I bought it at $22, expecting it to go up to $30. But instead, it immediately dropped to $17. Fortunately, there was another, last rise on the market, Yahoo went back up to $22 again, and I got out fast.

Mathematics of the market: 2x2 = 5-1

After six weeks, the Easter rally was over. The Nasdaq was as high as 2400 points; 50 percent higher than just a bit more than one month earlier! Some stocks reached new highs; others dropped, a typical reaction to a big oversold rally: some investors are waiting for the follow-through, others for more tumbling.

I considered some stocks overvalued and sold them short: first of all Qualcomm at $57. It shot up to $62 where I was squeezed, and then climbed slowly to $70 and stayed there for a few weeks. Then, in a few months, it tumbled to less than $40. So I had been right, but first everything happened upside down. The idea was right, but the timing was wrong. As Kostolany says, 2x2 is never 4; on the stock market, it is 5-1. In other words, if one expects something logical to happen, it will happen sooner or later, but first it can go the other way. Let's see why.

Suppose that a lot of traders considered Qualcomm to be overvalued at $57. They all sold it short (maybe others had sold short earlier as well). Seeing that the price wasn't falling as anticipated, some start closing the shorts. This sparks a rally, and all the others are squeezed out of the shorts positions. And this happens again and again until most shorts disappear. Than, all of a sudden, the price collapses.

What is the best course of action in a situation like this? In this example, a smart trader opens the shorts only when he sees that the stock can't exceed a certain price (the resistance) for a period of time, and not until the general market is in a downtrend; going against the general trend of the market can be very dangerous, as we will see.

Profit warning

In June, while the general market was still relatively high, I saw that Nokia was tumbling fast. After it had reached its top at €40 still in May, now it fell about one euro a day. At €34, I thought it had fallen too far and bought ten thousand shares, but it just remained there at about €34. I should have known that this was a bad sign. After such a fast fall, it should have jumped up. But I hoped...I didn't know what.

In cases like these, hoping is forbidden! Most traders hope that when a stock is going the wrong way it will turn, and when they have a winning position all these investors fear that the market can take back the profit at any time. So they keep the losing position, and cut the winning one. That's the surest way of losing money on the stock market. As Livermore says; one should keep the winning stocks and hope that the profit grows even bigger, and get out of the losing ones, fearing that the loss will increase.

That's what I should have done with Nokia, when I saw that it wasn't performing well, just slipping slowly downwards. I thought that the support at €32 would hold it, but there was something strange I had never seen before. While other stocks were flat or rising a bit, Nokia was always dumped in European trading. I suspected that it was some kind of insider selling. Unfortunately, my hope was stronger than my suspicions.

The stock soon fell to the support. It should have jumped, at least a bit, but it didn't. Then the company issued a profit warning. I would have never believed it! The stock fell immediately through the support, leaving a wide gap in a moment. It fell by €6, or more than 20%, before it stabilized. The overall market started to tumble as well. I sold my shares with an enormous loss. And it was a good decision: the share fell another 40% in the next two months.

And now, after this shocking experience, I realized that the system of warnings sharply increases the risk of any investment. After a warning, even a blue chip can fall 20-30% with a gap, so it's impossible to limit the loss. Without warnings, this would never happen on a sophisticated market; instead, the facts would be reflected in the price gradually, so investors had enough time to get out, or just trigger a stop-loss at any time. And, of course, a warning is a perfect opportunity for the insiders. They know it long before, so they have time to sell, even sell short. Who dumped those big quantities of shares of Nokia before the warning? Of course, insiders did. It was a brilliant opportunity for them to make extra money. The warning, as we could see later, was bullshit – the company had good earnings, as good as expected before the warning.

Besides the warnings, there's another manipulative thing; it is the upgrading and downgrading of equities by big brokerage houses. These often have the same effect: huge gaps and this way big risk for investors. And the opinion of the analysts changes fast: I experienced many times that the same stock or sector was upgraded, then in two weeks' time downgraded, then in another two weeks upgraded again. I think the stock markets would be more safe and investor-friendly if the system of warnings, upgrades and downgrades didn't exist, and this way insider trading would be less common as well.

The falling knives

During the summer, a new decline started. First it was slow, but there were some stocks that fell a lot in a very short period of time. I thought there must be a cover in these. Many people thought the same; they bought into the falling knives. The relief never came: these were mainly shares of companies approaching bankruptcy.

One of them was British telecom-equipment maker Marconi. The share had been trading at over £10 a year earlier, but now, after a warning, it fell from about £2.50 to £1. Many traders started to buy it, among them one of my brokers. In my experience it isn't a good sign when everyone buys a falling share, so I decided not to buy unless it went much lower. As I expected, it tumbled further. At 65 pence I bought shares, but it was still too early. It fell further, to almost zero; the bottom was 12 pence.

The other stock I traded unluckily was Exodus, the troubled US dot-com. First it fell to $1, and then in a few days shot up to $2.70. Then it tumbled again and at just over $1, I bought it. But it fell further, and in three days, it broke through the one-dollar barrier.

Fortunately I managed to sell it before it went down to zero. These 'penny stocks' can be quite dangerous because on a percentage basis they can move a lot. So if we buy a share at about or below one dollar (or euro), we should buy it like an option, acknowledging that the whole investment can be easily lost, or of course doubled or tripled in a best-case scenario.

In August, the selling pressure was increasing. Individual shares tumbled faster and faster. I should have been short of Qualcomm now, or other techs, such as Juniper or Ciena. Both had shot up from around $35 to $70 in the Easter rally and now fell under $20, and still there was nothing to stop them falling further.

In the first days of September all the major indices and almost all the individual stocks reached new lows. I bought into the falling knives once again: I bought Juniper at $13, but as the market fell further, I just wanted to get out. I was lucky; it snuck back up to $13 and I got out without a loss before it fell below $10.

I thought it had to be the last phase of heavy selling. Pessimism was growing; stocks became oversold. However, as I learned, the market can become more oversold before it turns.

In times like these, there are two different strategies to follow. Kostolany says that when the market gets oversold, the smart investor can start buying, but only gradually, keeping enough cash just in case. No matter when when the market turns, he just continues buying, even after the bottom, for a while. Then, after the first, furious rally, he stops buying and just waits, and sits on the shares until the market becomes overbought again.

But what if the investor doesn't have enough cash? He can't afford to buy downside; he could be forced out just before the market turns. Livermore says the smart investor buys only after the bottom, and continues buying upside. And how can we decide that the market has really turned?

First, we have to identify the last phase of the fall. In this phase, rallies don't last even a full trading day. The market is falling again in a few hours, and goes to new lows. In this phase, pessimism is overwhelming. Analysts, even the big names, predict further falls and create target prices well below the actual, already low rates, something they rarely do when prices are in the sky!

So when everything seems hopeless, all at once there are no more sellers. One or more stocks start rallying, against the trend. For a time, few believe that it's the turning point. But there are lots of bargain hunters waiting for the moment, and when they see that the sellers aren't coming any more, they all rush to buy. Prices shoot up 5-10% in minutes and never look back; there's not even a downtick, and if there is, the bulls catch the stock immediately. This lasts the whole day; the market closes near the daily high. The Dow skyrockets 2-300 points on days like these, and the S&P 500 and the Nasdaq rise at least 3%.

The next two days are crucial. On the second day there may be a slight pullback, but if it is followed by another big rally, then the direction of the least resistance has turned for a long time. And of course, the majority cannot recognize it: they talk about suckers' rally. As long as they don't believe it, the prices can only go up.

9/11

After the bearish days of early September, I felt that the turning point must be close. As I mentioned, it is impossible to guess the day or even the week of it; the investor must wait patiently, no matter how low the market goes. Maybe it would turn, but then something irregular happens...just as in this September.

I was impatient; I tried to catch the bottom. I bought Cisco at about $12, which seemed quite a low price, and 5000 shares of Nokia at €13. It jumped immediately a euro, where I took the profit, seeing that the overall market was still going down. However, I had a feeling with Nokia, similar to what I had had before the warning, but this time upside: the line of least resistance had changed.

The next morning, the share started rising again in Europe. I placed a bid one euro under the actual price, waiting for a dip. In early afternoon European time, my broker called and said that Nokia had held a press conference and painted a rosy picture about its future, less than three months after the warning. The share immediately jumped 2 euros and continued rising. I felt terrible; I regretted I hadn't bought at whatever price I could in the morning.

And then, 20 minutes later, the broker called again and said that just before the press conference, someone had dumped shares, without any price limit, and I got my shares, but he hadn't noticed it on the Instinet trading platform earlier. So I had bought at €14, and the actual price was €17 by then! I was thrilled. Unfortunately, my happiness didn't last long.

That afternoon, I was to meet the general manager of the brokerage company where I traded (a friend of mine since the compensation note business). I had just stepped into his office when the news came that one tower of the World Trade Center in New York was burning. At first we didn't pay much attention, but in about ten minutes, the atmosphere became tenser. We went to the dealing room just in time to see the second plane crash into the other tower.

Panic started to arise; the traders kept one eye on the share prices that were just starting to fall, and the other eye on CNN. I did the same. In a few minutes the third plane had crashed into the Pentagon. I immediately sold Nokia, but the giant profit had already melted down to almost zero. Then the first tower collapsed. Everybody in the dealing room, including me, was shocked. I completely forgot my Cisco shares. By the time I remembered about them, trading on American markets was suspended.

After the first shock, we started to discuss the situation. Some traders overestimated the possibilities of

Adventurous moneymaking

the terrorists and expected a world war, considering the terrorist attack a second Pearl Harbor. My opinion was, and I convinced the chief trader, that the enemy, whoever it was, could not be strong enough to disturb the present world order. The world economy would survive, and of course equities markets, too.

US markets were closed for another three days. In Europe stock exchanges were open, but there wasn't heavy selling; the markets were all waiting for their 'older brother', Wall Street. There was one share that did not fall at all: Nokia. On the contrary, it climbed up to €17, where it had been just before the terrorist attacks.

The next Monday, US markets re-opened. Despite an immediate rate cut, there was a relentless dumping of all the shares. All the indices went below their April lows, and the Dow fell under 9000 points for the first time since the Russian crisis. The free-fall lasted the whole week. The Dow tumbled about 200 points each day, the S&P 500 fell below 1000 points, testing the lows of the Russian crisis. The Nasdaq dropped to 1390 points, losing 75% of its peak value during just a year and a half.

What caused this incredible selling panic? The US and the world seemed to survive the terrorist attacks. I think it was psychology, the most dominant factor on the market in the short term. Insurance companies dumped all the shares they had been carefully collecting in the previous years. They thought they would have to pay enormous sums because of possible future attacks. Investors, among them institutions, thought that air traffic would decrease, that people would stop flying, so they got rid of all shares of airliners, sometimes at half or third of the pre-attack prices. They were wrong, of course. And a lot of investors dumped stocks just because they thought it was the end of the world.

The turning point

On Friday, the trend seemed to turn. In the morning, European markets still tumbled to unbelievable lows. The Dow also opened sharply lower, but after an hour, the sellers disappeared. During the next five hours of the trading, the Dow surged more than 400 points! European markets also turned immediately and soared about 4-5 percent in the last hour before they closed. However, tech stocks still remained flat and dropped again next Monday.

On Tuesday, all markets opened higher. After about 20 minutes, something happened I had never seen before. Data stopped coming across the screen. Then just a flash: each share was about 5% higher. Then there was no data again for a few minutes. The next flash: another 5%! Then in a minute, data was flowing normally, but the market was 10% higher than it had been five minutes earlier. What could have happened?

Everybody realized that this was the turning point; everybody wanted to buy at the same time. Prices immediately jumped and data couldn't be transmitted because of the irregularly large volume of stocks being traded in such a short period of time. And the skyrocketing continued. There was no pullback: by the end of the day, some techs were 10-20% higher! Ciena and Juniper, my favorites, shot up from $9 to $12-13, and Cisco also joined the rally that was so furious that I dared not buy 15-20% higher. However, this was the day an investor *must* buy, at any price, any moment. On such an oversold market, if it turns like that, the rally doesn't just last for days, but for weeks. This time it lasted *3 months!*

As I was sure that we were at the beginning of a big oversold rally, I decided to buy shares the next day. I had target prices for some stocks: for Nokia €20, for Ciena and Juniper $20 each. Nokia opened at €18, only €2 from my target and Juniper opened at $15, 60% higher than two days earlier: I didn't want to buy them after such a fast rally so close to the target. Ciena was between $13 and $14, so I decided to buy it, and keep it until $20, if possible. First it fell back to $12.50, but after a few days it rose again, as I had expected.

One day, after trading hours, Juniper released its earnings. It was neither very good nor a surprise, but the price immediately jumped from $17 to $20. It had reached my target in only two days. I thought it had gone too far (up 100% in a week), and too fast, so still the same day after market hours I sold short 10,000 shares. The next day it opened higher, at about $21. Then it dropped to $20, but there were a lot of buyers there. I immediately closed the shorts with a minimal loss. It proved to be a good idea, as the share jumped to $27 in another week.

Three months later Juniper was under $10. What had happened? It seemed logical that surging to $20 from $10 in a week is too much, especially for a stock of a fundamentally weak company. Many investors shared this opinion, so they all sold short. But those who had sold short at lower prices were squeezed out so they had to buy. The price rose, those who shorted at $20 were also squeezed (like me), and so on in a spiral. Of course the short sellers were right later, when the price fell so low, but at first they lost out. What should they have done? Just wait until the trend was changing and then act. They were right but first it was upside down. Like always on the stock market; 2x2 = 5-1.

At the same time, a week after the bottom, small-caps joined the rally. Investors were searching desperately for any stocks that still hadn't risen a lot. These are the less liquid stocks so they can jump even bigger when hungry investors find them, even if these are shares in bankrupt companies.

Marconi (Trade of the year)

A colleague of mine called and excitedly said that in his opinion, Marconi was going to jump. It was trading at about 15p for days before it started to go up slowly, and then at 18p my friend bought 1 million shares. The next day as he saw his hunch was right, he bought

Adventurous moneymaking

another million shares at about 20p. He bought on margin with only about £150,000 in his account, but in this way he was able to buy for £380,000.

Still that same day (!), the stock skyrocketed to 28p. The next trading day it rose to 33p, and in another day it reached 50p!

It would have been the trade of the year – if my friend had sold in time. But he got greedy, expecting 100 or even 200p. Such a giant profit must be taken, no matter what. It would've been £600,000, or about one million dollars, return on a three-day investment of £120,000. Not many investors have the courage and the skills to do that!

I joined my friend but only at 29p with a hundred thousand shares, and sold at 45p. I suggested him to secure his incredible profit while I took my relatively small one (£16,000), but he didn't want to sell that day. Then he made a much bigger mistake: he just let the price gradually come down for another few days, without making a profit lock-in. He should have decided that he wouldn't let it go below a certain price; let's say 45 or 40, or even 35p. He ended up selling at 28p, still a good profit, two hundred thousand pounds (one third of the possible profit if he sold in time).

By that time, most stocks and indices had reached their pre- 9/11 levels, among them the airliners which had been dumped in the first days of panic. It was obvious even a few weeks after the attacks that passengers would not be terrorized, they would continue to fly. So did the prices of airliner shares.

The 'Taliban rally'

In October, when the US launched a war against the Taliban in Afghanistan, the market cheered the war and prices continued climbing. Nothing could stop them, not even the anthrax letters in the US; the more bad news there was, the bigger the surge in prices. The reason, as we saw earlier, was that those who found that the market had gone too high sold short, and when they saw that there was no heavy selling after bad news, started to close immediately. Not to mention all those investors, among them funds, who were sitting in cash and wanted to join the rally.

I found a share, a good old one, AMD, still staying near the bottom. It stood just under $10, after bottoming at $8. I bought some, with a target of $15, but it didn't rise for a few more days. I thought it was a dog and sold furiously. I should have been patient: in a few days it surged to $15, then up to $20...

There was another laggard, a near-bankrupt penny stock, McLeod. It had tumbled from $3 to 30-40 cents in the previous months, so I expected some correction. One day the company had some comments about its rosy outlooks and the price surged still pre-market. I bought at 60 cents, sure it would go up to 80-90. I sold it the same day at 85 cents, making a good profit (25 cents a share, but it is 40% in case of such a penny share!) In the next few days I made some more day trades with it. Later it started to sag again, and considering a bargain, I bought some shares at 23 cents. It was a mistake; despite its earlier rosy comments, the company filed for bankruptcy and I was only able to offload the shares at about 5 cents.

In early December, the rally was still going on. The Nasdaq reached 2000 points, the Dow nearly 10,000, and the S&P 1170 points. My darling Nokia surged to not only €20 as I expected, but over €30! When Ciena reached my target, $20, I sold it, making a 65% profit.

Six weeks after the rally began, some stocks were showing signs of exhausting. I started short selling, especially two shares, PMC-Sierra and German chipmaker Infineon. PMC-Sierra was $10 at the bottom, and now $27. The company made no profit, and its future was not too rosy, so $27 seemed a bit much.

One day I sold 5000 shares short at $27.50, but in an hour it went up to 28. I didn't care, I thought there was no way it could go much higher. I left the market and went to the cinema. During the film, my broker called, frightened because the price had gone up to $29. I told him to sell another 5000 shares at $29, and if it went higher, 5000 more at $30. The broker thought I got crazy. I switched off my mobile phone and enjoyed the film... When I left the cinema I called the broker; the price was $28. In the last 30 minutes before the closing bell I was following the trading: PMC-Sierra dropped to $27, where I bought back all the 10,000 shares with a small profit. Had I listened to my broker, I would have lost $10,000!

Over the next few days, the stock traded at about $27-28, so I stopped shorting it. Instead, I tried Infineon on the German market. Its fundamentals were only a little better than that of PMC-Sierra, so I sold several times short at €27, but it just stayed there so I left it as well.

In mid-December, the long awaited correction arrived. There was one day when both Infineon and PMC-Sierra tumbled 15%. Unfortunately, I didn't have any shorts... What would have been the right thing to do? Buying put options, as we will see.

Three days before Christmas I went on a skiing trip to France. While I was there I didn't follow the market. I thought nothing interesting would happen during the Christmas week, but I was wrong. When I got home on the last day of the year, the market was sharply higher.

7. BOTTOM FISHING

Put options experiment

In the first three days of 2002, the rally continued, with stocks and indices going at least as high as they had been at the top a month earlier. In these days, I read a lot about the effect of the first trading days of a year. In some opinions, if there's a rally in the first five days of January, there will be a bull market that year, and if January is bullish/bearish, then the whole year is bullish/bearish. To tell the truth, I never believed these superstitious things. If they were true, all the investors would rush to exploit the possibility, and this way it would be a *fait accompli*. After a bullish January, everybody would buy as much shares as they could afford, and would want to take their profits in the last month of the year, which itself would cause a big slump.

So after the big rally of the first days, analysts predicted a bull market for the whole year and I became bearish again. I set up targets for the individual shares: $30 for Qualcomm (then $55), $13 for Juniper, $15 for PMC-Sierra (both $27 then), and $40 for Microsoft ($65-70 then). The reasons were simple: Juniper and PMC-Sierra were loss makers, so I thought they were quite expensive over $20. Qualcomm and Microsoft were fundamentally overvalued, with a P/E over 30: I thought no share could remain so overpriced after two years of a bear market. These shares remained high because of the flight to quality; funds dumped shares that fell a lot and escaped to others, mainly big-cap blue chips, which hadn't fallen much yet. Maybe they were convinced that these would never fall, or maybe they just wanted to show their clients what strong stocks they held, but sooner or later, the bear reaches each share...

Now, instead of shorting stocks, I decided to buy put options. Thus, paying a certain amount, I had the right to sell stocks at a certain price anytime until expiry. The advantage of this was that I couldn't be squeezed out no matter how high the share might rise. However, there's a serious problem with options: the pressure of time. If the share price isn't going in the expected direction fast enough, the option expires worthless (or lower than the price we bought). For longer expiry, premiums are quite high, and if the investor renews the options after expiry (buys the same option for the next expiry), the sums of the premiums add up, so the risk increases.

Premiums for volatile PMC-Sierra were too expensive, but for Qualcomm, they seemed reasonable. The share was $55, and I thought sooner or later it would go down to $30, but even short term to $45. I bought options at a strike price of $55 for January for a premium of $1.70. The stock first went up to $62, but at least I didn't have to worry, I couldn't lose more than $1.70 a share. At the expiry, it was $53, so I just got back the premium.

I renewed the options for new expiries, and the stock continued declining. Next month it was $45, and later it tumbled to $30. My target was right! However, I had to wait almost a half year altogether, and pay the premiums again and again, so while the stock fell $25, I made a profit of only 10$ a share. (Still quite nice!)

Bull trap

In the second half of January and the first weeks of February, the general market was sliding slowly. There was a share, Q-Logic, at about $50 which I thought was quite high, with earnings slightly higher than $1 a share. I sold it short at $50 several times. It started to fall each time but after falling 2-3 dollars it immediately surged again, so I covered the shorts at about $47-48, and opened them again at $50. I repeated this trade six or seven times. After a time, the price started to stay at $50. I stopped shorting, and in a few days it surged to $57.

Why had this happened with that particular share? Maybe it was too obvious for too many investors that the share was overvalued so all of them shorted it. They were waiting for the fall impatiently, and when it didn't come fast enough, they covered, just like me. There could be many short positions, and perhaps the real sellers knew it, so they stopped selling at lower prices. After a time, when the market got lower but this stock remained high, more and more short sellers 'attacked' the share. The other sellers, seeing their shares overperforming, stopped selling, and a short squeeze was coming.

Then, at the end of February, maybe the short sellers gave up and closed all their positions. The buying pressure disappeared, so the price started to decline. It fell to $45 slowly, and now crashed to $36 in two days.

The whole market seemed weak; I expected a big decline, so sold Intel short at $30, Veritas Software at $37 and Infineon at €27. There was only one strange thing I didn't pay enough attention to: the Dow was quite high at 10,000 points, and didn't fall a point...

Just as I opened my shorts, instead of the expected falling, the market started rallying. First only the Dow, but later all shares joined the rally. It seemed a huge short squeeze. I hoped that it would last only one day, so I kept my shorts, but the rally went on for another five days.

During this short period, brokerage firms upgraded some shares, fuelling the rally. Analysts, among them big names, even predicted a new bull market. That was the moment I knew that it was one of the the biggest bull trap I'd ever seen. On the sixth day of the rally, my brokerage company prohibited short positions. Why? Nobody knows...

Maybe they believed the new everlasting bull theory, and thought it would better if investors didn't sell short. That was a good sign of the sentiment. I told them they could be sure that the day of their decision would be the top of the market for a long time, and of course it was. The S&P 500 stood at the January high at 1170 points, the Nasdaq at 2000 points, forming a double top, and the Dow exceeded its previous high.

The next day the market started to tumble, and the downturn lasted for five long months! At the and of July, the S&P 500 was only 760 points, and the Nasdaq had lost half of its March value...

I didn't have time to open the shorts at other brokerage firms because after settling and transferring the money, prices were already sharply lower. Instead I bought put options, but due to recent market volatility, premiums were quite expensive, so the profit from them was even less than the loss of the shorts.

At the top, when I had to close out the shorts, Intel was $34.50, Veritas $44, Infineon €29. At the end of July, Intel and Veritas were both $15, Infineon fell below €10! Of course I wouldn't have kept the shorts until then, but one thing is sure: I would have kept my Infineon shorts until it plummeted to €13, my target. That was the biggest disappointment. Sometimes, in between, I sold Infineon short and made some profit, but missed the big money.

So, as we can see, the rally in early March was an enormous bull trap. I was right when I expected the sell-off, but first everything was upside down. As is so often the case on the stock market; 2x2 is 5-1. The market downturn was obvious so many investors sold short, which resulted first in a short squeeze. And when it was over and many others were expecting a new bull market and went long, the market collapsed.

Under the 'Osama lows'

Not only did the market collapse; it simply couldn't stop falling. The tumble lasted for five months without a correction. And, for the bulls' biggest surprise, the main indices fell to the 'Osama-lows', the levels the market had bottomed at soon after the 9/11 terrorist attacks, when the S&P 500 was at 950 points, the Nasdaq at about 1400 points and the Dow at 8200 points. And that wasn't the bottom this time! The bear market went on; the S&P tumbled 200, the Nasdaq 300 more points.

During this time, I bought into falling knives on two occasions. One was Verisign; it had come down from over $40 to $18 in a relatively short period of time. I bought it at about $16, but the next day, after a profit warning, it tumbled to $10, and two days later to $8 (see Figure 11, page 254). Once again, the system of profit warnings had increased the risk for the investors to an enormous level; there was a 30% decline in one day and further drops in the next trading days for a stock which has a volume of several million shares a day. Later, Verisign rebounded to $11 but then fell again to $5 in the summer.

My other 'falling knife' was graphic chipmaker Nvidia (see Figure 10, page 250). In the bull trap, it was over $50, but by the summer it had fallen to $16. Then it rebounded to $23 but then tumbled again. At $20 I bought 3000 shares for day trade, but it proved to be a mistake; it immediately slipped to $19. I decided to wait and hope, one of the biggest mistakes a trader can make. One should never ever be stuck to a position opened for day trade! No matter how painful it is, it must be closed out the same day. But on this occasion I didn't follow my own rule...

The next day Nvidia opened at $18 and fell further sharply. It tumbled fast to $15.50. There, hazardously, I decided to buy 3000 more shares, expecting an intraday rebound. The rebound came, and the share slowly climbed a dollar. This time the day trade was ingenious! I sold the new 3000 shares and took the loss on 1000 of the original 3000. Why only 1000? I didn't want to take more loss than the profit on the day trade, which of course was foolish. The loss should have been cut, the sooner the better.

The stock fell further next day, but the day after, an analyst made a good comment on it. Huge buyers emerged and I joined them at $15.30. The share rose slowly; there were still a lot of sellers. Then I closed the successful day trade at $16.40 and five minutes before the closing bell I sold 1000 of my remaining 2000 shares.

And what a clever decision! After the market close, there was a warning or a downgrade, I don't remember. In that moment I knew that this share was over. It could be another Verisign...and it really was. The next day, pre-market, it was trading at $12.70. I immediately sold the last 1000 shares. It fell further fast, closing at $11 that day, $10 the next day and $8.50 two days later...

Yes, a stock, tumbling from 50 to 8 dollars in 3-4 months... What a money making opportunity by short selling, and what a mistake to buy into it anywhere, no matter how much it had already fallen!

Bargain hunting

In July, the market became incredibly oversold. My favorite, Nokia was under €11 which earlier would have seemed impossible. It was so low that I decided to buy almost each day for a day trade. I found the risk limited; a bellwether like Nokia is unlikely to drop quickly into single-digit territory. I had small gains on the day trades.

On a certain day, European markets fell heavily; it was clearly a capitulation day. I started to buy Nokia again at €10.80, but it fell further. I continued buying at €10.55 still before the US opening. Then American markets opened with a gap down; everything seemed hopeless. But after about half an hour, the dumping ceased for a few minutes, then there was a last selling attempt and when it failed, a furious rally started and lasted through the day. I sold my ten thousand Nokia shares with a nice profit, and a bit later, I realized that this was a clear bottom day. I decided to buy something instead of the wasted Nokia: in a dip I bought Microsoft at about $43. I sold it at $44.80 in an hour. Just too early: when the market closed, it was $46, and the next day $49...

And Nokia soared to €15, in just a week. Of course, I should have kept my shares, Nokia and Microsoft both. The investor should always let the profits keep growing and cut the losses immediately. This was a deeply oversold market; it was obvious that a strong rally would last more than one day.

About a week later, one evening after the market close I looked at the screen and saw that Cisco was rising furiously on the Instinet trading platform, on which shares can be traded before and after the regular trading hours; its earnings had been better than expected. The closing price was $12, now trading at $12.50. It didn't fall back in an hour, so I decided to buy 5000 shares. It climbed to $13 still after hours!

I figured it wouldn't open lower the next day not only because of the good earnings, but also because the share had been dumped for weeks, and despite the general market rise in the last week, it had fallen to new lows. So there had been heavy selling, and in case of an oversold stock, unexpected good news usually ignites a rally (and vice versa: if the share is rising before the earnings release and the earnings are worse than expected, it often falls afterwards).

As I expected, the stock surged to $13.40 before it retreated. When it came back to $13, I bought another 5000 shares. Then it fell further, to $12.70. It seemed as if the rally was over. I had ten thousand shares, at an average price of $12.75. I didn't want to let it go much below that level of course, so I sold when it looked up a bit and started to decline again, at about $12.85.

My decision seemed right: on that same day it fell to $12.40. The whole market seemed to turn down.

But still in the last hour, it suddenly turned again and surged until the closing bell. It was such a heavy reversal that I thought that a serious rally would surely follow, so I bought some Nokia instead of Cisco, which I was shaken off. And yes, there was a big rally in the next weeks: Cisco rose to over $15.

What were the consequences of this Cisco trade? Why was I shaken off? Why did the share fall back so much before rising further? The explanation is simple. The general market had been rising for a week, so a pullback was normal anytime. And that, of course, could hurt Cisco. Considering that it was not the beginning of the rally, I should have been satisfied with a limited profit, and sold the original 5000 shares instead of buying another 5000. Or I could have sold even earlier, still at $13.30, when the share was 10% higher than its closing price the previous day. For a bellwether like Cisco, 10% is quite a huge movement.

The rally lasted five weeks after the July low. In the first 3-4 weeks, lots of pessimistic comments could be heard and read. I think a lot of shorts had been building up during the five-month tumble, and it was closing them that fuelled the rally.

In the sixth week, American markets started to slide, first slowly, then in the middle of September, much faster. Now the Dow was the fastest tumbling index; it soon reached 7500 points, the famous double bottom level in the Russian crisis, while the S&P 500 was still above the July lows. Dow component bellwethers like JP Morgan and General Electric led the fall: GE lost half of its value in a year, JPM fell below $18, its July low. I bought there, but it didn't stop falling, so I jumped out.

European stocks fell even faster. My beloved Infineon was in single-digit territory! It was so painful to think about the missed profit on my shorts from €28...

The German market tumbled well below its July low. It was unbelievable; how low could it go? The DAX, which had been at 8000 points in the year 2000, was a bit above 2500 points, less than a third of its peak. If the broad US market would have fallen as much as the German, the Dow would have been under 4000 points and the S&P 500 less than 500 points!

It's an interesting question why European (first of all German) stocks fell to fundamentally cheap levels while US markets didn't. One possible explanation is that interest rates in the US became much lower than those in Europe so more money remained on the stock market. And maybe investors, seeing the US markets performing better, redirected their investments from Europe to the US.

So looking for a cheap deal, I started to buy German stocks, even before the market bottom. One of them was good old Infineon. My downside target had been €13 when it was almost €30; now I bought at €7.50. It couldn't even jump to €8, so I sold it at about €7.70. And what a clever decision! In a few days, I could buy it at €6, and even €5.50...

Bottom fishing

The other stock I bought at this time was the great European reinsurance company, Munich Re. It had fallen down from over €300 a year earlier, and dropped from €170 almost without an up-tick. I thought, as a giant insurance company, it could not be another Verisign or Nvidia, not to mention Marconi (which in the meantime went bankrupt and fell to 1 penny). When it was €100, I expected a major cover, to about €150.

One morning in early October, the German market started to rise furiously. Munich Re shot up from €97 to €107. It was the first sign of the approaching rally. When it fell back still during the day, I bought shares at €103 and some more at €101 and waited for the rally.

The final US bottom

Meanwhile, stocks in the US tumbled further. The Dow fell to 7200, the Nasdaq to almost 1000 points, losing 80% of its peak value 2 and a half years earlier! The S&P 500 fell once again to 760 points, the July low. One day, it fell even below: it seemed that the support was broken. But after half an hour, it turned and soon reached 760 points again. Many participants thought it might only be a retest of the new resistance, but it soon went higher. The breakdown was false; an incredibly strong buying power emerged and prices jumped 3-5% immediately, like so many times before on the deeply oversold market.

Adventurous moneymaking

On the phone with friends and colleagues, we all agreed it had to be the bottom. I told one of them I thought the rally would last at least six weeks. Of course I rushed to buy something: I chose JP Morgan, Nokia and QLogic. Unfortunately, JP Morgan and Q-Logic didn't perform that first day, so I sold them, and bought GE instead. It was down to $21 and the earnings release came on the next day. As I'd learned from experience, if a bellwether like GE tumbles so much before it, it can do nothing but skyrocket after the earnings release, and that was the case this time. The next day, before the market opened, the earnings were released, in line with expectations. The price jumped over $24; I sold my shares at $24.50.

My Munich Re, bought a bit over €100, performed wonderfully. On the first day of the rally, it closed at €109. The next day it rose to €120, and the following week went up to €150. It reached my target in a week!

J.P. Morgan, which I couldn't buy low enough, soon reached $20. Earlier, still in the darkest days, there had been market rumors about the bankruptcy of the company. These were so widespread and convincing that some funds stopped buying the stock and brokerage firms suggested avoiding it. But who released such rumors? Maybe some clever analysts and traders; maybe there was a pool which started circulating it, waited until the share price tumbled deep down, and then bought all the shares from those who believed the rumors. In the circumstances of general pessimism, after share prices had been tumbling for almost half year, it would be easy to do. I regret that I didn't keep some stocks after I had heard the rumor. I knew that if it proved to be false, nothing but an enormous rally could come, and that was indeed the case; JP Morgan was selling at $25 in November and $28 a few weeks later! It almost doubled its price from the bottom, which is very rare in case of a Dow component, especially in such a short period of time.

The other stock I bought near the bottom but jumped out when I saw that it wasn't performing on the same day was QLogic. It was the share that simply couldn't come down from $50 for long, but in the last phase of the bear market (which is the fastest), it fell to $20 in a few weeks. Now, on the next day of the bull run, after I had sold it, the share rose sharply to $24. And then came the better-than-expected earnings. It jumped 20% the next day, soon reached and exceeded $30, and in another month it was over $40...

Bumpy ride

The rally lasted for eight weeks, longer than I had predicted, but it wasn't an easy ride. The first phase was fast: the Dow quickly jumped 1000 points, the S&P 500 a hundred points. But when the latter reached 900 points (about 20% from the bottom), it seemed as if there was an endless sell-program at that level. Every time it printed at 900 points, it immediately fell back. But after a few days it fell back less and less, it started to stick to 900, and at the same time, a lot of individual shares, mainly on the Nasdaq, went to new highs. It seemed that the demand was stronger, but the market still didn't want to exceed the resistance at 900 points.

Then one morning some GDP, unemployment and other figures were released. The figures were terrible and the market first fell, but for only a few minutes. Then those who desperately wanted to buy (either the shorts or those who feared missing the bull run), saw that there wasn't any more selling pressure even after the bad news, and started to buy vehemently. The S&P 500 broke through the 900-point barrier, and this was followed by an enormous rally. Shares of loss-making companies joined the rally with incredible speed. AMD and PMC-Sierra surged from $3 to over $8; in the case of PMC-Sierra, there was a big short squeeze.

In that phase investors were desperately looking for shares still near the bottom. Of course they found Verisign and Nvidia: Verisign climbed slowly from $4 to $7, and then surged quickly to over $10. Nvidia, catching the bottom at $7-8, stayed under $10 for weeks and then in three days it shot up to $16.

After this furious rally, the first pullback arrived. The surging shares fell back fast: PMC-Sierra to $5, Nvidia to $10. The pullback lasted less than a week, then the rally continued. Comments became bullish: even a star analyst, who had been predicting the end of the world just six weeks earlier, was now talking about the new bull market again. Optimism was growing and many funds wanted to join the ride; they spent almost all their cash to get in on the rally. In the last days of November the newspapers and financial websites were full of the expressions 'Santa Claus rally' and 'Year-end rally'. Everyone bought to the limit, expecting these rallies. But later, when they wanted to take the profits, who would have bought? Nobody, of course.

The market top was on December 1. The S&P 500 reached 960 points, the Dow was over 9000 points for a few minutes, and the Nasdaq approached 1500 points; a huge, 50% rise in eight weeks. And then there was a slide from the very first day of December to the very last. Hope stayed alive all month; if there was an uptick, the next minute there was a comment about the possible 'Santa rally', which of course never came. In one month, the S&P 500 slipped back 10%.

European capitulation

In the first 2 weeks of January 2003, there was a rally again, fuelled by money that some companies paid to their pension funds. Approximately $100 billion poured into these funds, but of course only a part of it went to the stock market and when it had been spent, another downturn started in mid-January.

European markets were the leaders in the tumble, once again. The German DAX fell to its previous low of 2500 points, the Footsie went to new six-year lows. As the stock prices plummeted, the value of the portfolios of some institutions, mainly insurance companies, fell to a point where they decided they had to sell, to have enough cash just in case. This is called *forced selling*.

But how is it possible that they got to this point? Hadn't they thought about this possibility a bit earlier? Or, rather years earlier, still when prices were in the sky? Unfortunately, they were, like so many others, blinded by the hopes of the everlasting bull market. And when prices came down to dangerous levels, they closed their eyes and hoped that the market wouldn't drop further. But it did.

Of course, shares of insurance companies suffered most. My darling Munich Re. soon fell back to €100, the level I had caught the 50% rally four months earlier. I thought this level would be a strong support, so I bought the share once again. It wasn't; the stock only rose to 103 slowly, so I sold it. It soon fell to 94, the previous low in October, and I bought again, but it didn't jump so I got out again. Then it tumbled to 74 in less than a week.

It was quite interesting how it was turning then, a good example for how the line of least resistance changes. As it descended from €100 to 74, there were sharp but short rallies. These never lasted more than one day, and afterwards the price tumbled again and again with enormous volume; the stock couldn't take a breath. But on the day when it reached its bottom at €74, it closed a bit higher, and the next day opened at €77. In the next 3 days, in the first 20-30 minutes of the trading it dropped again, but then a rally emerged and lasted the whole day: three positive reversals in a row! That's a bullish sign; the line of least resistance has turned. On the fourth day, it opened at €83 and surged to €88, and a day later to €93.50, testing the former low, which now became a resistance level.

As we can see, in the first three days, going up and down in a narrow range, the share shook off almost everybody who wanted to catch the rally (among them me, I bought at €75 and 77, and sold at €79.40, still a good profit). Then in the next two days it could rise more quickly because the selling pressure disappeared.

The Saddam turmoil

From the previous autumn there had been more and more fuss about Iraq and Saddam Hussein. At first, as the market was rising, nobody cared. But in December, when stock prices were falling, the possible war against Iraq started being mentioned as a reason for the market slide. During the early January rally, it was forgotten again. But from the middle of January, when markets declined once more, the war became the main reason. As the reader can remember, there was a huge rally in 2001 during the war in Afghanistan, just weeks after the 9/11 terrorist attacks. Even the anthrax attacks against individuals and institutions in the US couldn't stop stock prices rising. On the contrary, as buyers saw that there was no supply even after the bad news, they rushed desperately for the stocks.

Adventurous moneymaking

So is war or the possibility of a war really bad for the stock market? Of course it used to be, during world wars or the American Civil War. But nowadays, when wars are local and far away, only terrorist attacks can threaten our countries. So, in my opinion, now there's absolutely no connection between the market direction and the wars in countries far away.

The war is always just a convenient explanation. If the market is falling, everybody wants to find a reason for this, and they find war. If there is a rally, nobody would mention war fears, just as during the war in Afghanistan. What is important isn't peace or war, but the mood of the investors and their expectations. And if there's a decline, it has its own causes, but the explanation of 'war fears' may seem easier or more comfortable. In this case, it was only the uncertainty about whether or not there would be a war that made the markets nervous. It lasted until the beginning of March when it became obvious that there would be war, with or without UN approval, and Saddam and his regime would be removed. The tug of war about Iraq had lasted so long that now everybody cheered the end of the uncertainty, supporters and opponents as well. And of course the stock market cheered too.

Still in the last days before the first shots, stocks tumbled once more. The S&P 500 fell to 780 points, the Dow to 7300, almost reaching their previous bottom. However, the Nasdaq was over 1200 points, much higher than in October: the tech sector started to show some relative strength, for the first time in three years.

The biggest slump took place in Europe, especially on my favorite, the German market. The DAX now fell below 2500 points and didn't stop tumbling. At that point, I bought my 'liebling', Munich Re at its previous bottom, €74. But the price didn't stop falling for even a second, it dropped further into uncharted territory, as did the benchmark, falling that day to 2400 points. The next day was the same: Munich Re sagged to €70, the DAX once again 100 points, to 2300. And then, one more terrible day: Munich Re crashed to €63, the DAX to 2200 points. Big names just tumbled like stones: pharmaceutical Bayer AG, car makers BMW and Volkswagen, the other insurance giant Allianz, chip maker Infineon, and big financials like Deutsche Bank and Hypovereinsbank. I told my broker that I predicted a big rise in the wake of such selling; the DAX would soon reach 4000 points! It took almost one year to reach that target.

8. BULL MARKET AGAIN

The final European bottom

That same day, when European stocks hit rock bottom, American markets also tumbled first, but turned in the afternoon. The next morning, European markets opened slightly higher. There were no more sellers after days of relentless dumping, but the buyers were still cautious. I recognized the moment – after all I had seen it so many times earlier – as the turning point. As I was sitting in deep losses with Munich Re, I dared open only small positions. I decided to buy DAXEX, the share of the fund containing the DAX constituents. I planned to keep it until the DAX reached my goal of 4000 points, as I was sure that we were beyond the bottom for a long time, if not forever. I'd never seen such a final sale on a developed market before!

Prices rose steeply later the day, in Europe and America as well, except one stock: Munich Re. The stock was so damaged it still couldn't rise on the first day. But the next day the DAX soared another 100 points, just as it had tumbled some days earlier. Munich Re opened at €65, in 20 minutes it was at €70, and in an hour, €75. I sold it at break-even, but the rise didn't stop there. It closed at €78 the next day, retreated to €74, and in another few days, it soared all the way to €90.

As we can see, the last few days of the fall were the fastest, and the first period of the counter-reaction was even faster! Buying early can cause enormous losses in this last phase of such an oversold market. But if an investor recognizes the turning point and buys just then, he can make huge profits in days or weeks.

When I had a nice gain of more than 3 euros on DAXEX (300 points in the DAX), I took the profit. It seemed logical to sell an index-related stock when the index had risen 15% in a few days, but either I should have kept it until it reached my target (ten months later), or I should have bought it again, in the first fallback. I missed it.

These first days of the rising market were the first days of the Iraq war, as well. Uncertainty was over; there was no doubt about the toppling of Saddam. The price of crude oil fell sharply, fuelling the stock market rally, which was enormous, just as in every V-shaped turn. The S&P 500 shot up to 900, the Dow to 8500 points, more than 15% each, in just ten days time.

After about a week the first pullback arrived. The DAX gave back more than half of its quick profit (from 2700 to 2400 points), but there were two stocks that tumbled to new lows. These were the two German insurer-giants, Allianz and Munich Re. As the latter reached €63, I bought it, saying that it wouldn't hit new lows on a rising market. But it did. In three days' time, it had fallen down to €50. Once again, I had to watch my stocks losing 10% every day. At the same time, Allianz tumbled to €40.

What happened? On April 1, I read the answer: the two companies had decided to sell a big part of shares in each other during the last days of the first quarter of the year. Why did they do it? Wasn't it silly to dump the stocks at the lowest possible prices? Maybe they were afraid of further falls on the market. A few weeks later, they could have easily sold at and over €80; there was a market for any quantity of shares at that high!

Fighting the trend

From the first day of April, the rally continued on each market; it was strong and broad-based. The leader was the tech sector, and the strongest the Internet stocks, just as had been the case four years earlier. Yahoo jumped from $20 to $30: it finally reached my target, two years after I had first set it – and it was down to $8 in between. Now the market justified expectations; the price not only reached, but later exceeded my target, soaring to $50 and higher (then it was split 2:1). Where had I gone wrong? I had correctly picked out the company as promising, but had misguidedly waited for a rise when the market itself was still in a downtrend; an individual stock can rarely go against the general market for long.

Bull market again

This first period of the bull market lasted until June. Until then, it could have been another bear rally. To tell the truth, at first I thought it was and considered the market worth short selling. I decided to open short positions on the German market, as it seemed the most overbought in the short term. In June, in the week of the triple witching (when options and futures expire), prices started to sag. I thought most of the open short positions would expire on triple witching day on Friday, thus prices could fall more steeply the next week. So on Friday, before the closing bell, I sold Munich Re and SAP short. When I saw that Monday's market confirmed the wisdom of this move, I sold some more SAP, 2 euros lower. The stocks tumbled that day, but the next day I felt that the least resistance had started to change, so I closed the shorts, securing a nice profit.

In the next 2 months, I sold SAP, Munich Re, Allianz and Infineon short several times. I had to close most with a small profit or small loss, as there was simply no market direction. It was the same on US markets: the S&P 500 hovered between 950 and 1000, the Nasdaq between 1600 and 1750 points.

I developed a theory: there had been a market plunge in summer and September and a big rally from October to December in the past six years, since the Asian Contagion. Why wouldn't the market do the opposite this year, and fall from October? If that were the case, then first there would be a rally still in September. And there was: the S&P 500 broke through 1000 points and the Nasdaq surged to 1900 points.

At the end of September, prices turned south, as I expected. I was sure this was the beginning of a big October to year-end fall. I sold Intel short as well as Infineon, Munich Re and SAP on the German market, and bought put options for Yahoo and DAXEX. At first everything was all right. Prices tumbled, especially on the German market: the DAX fell back from 3700 to 3200 points, SAP from €124 to €102 and Munich Re from €100 to €80. I thought I could sit on the shorts and just wait, until the market is becoming deeply oversold.

The bull is real!

It never happened. On the first day of October, heavy buying started on Wall Street. The beginning rally was so strong that I suddenly understood that this was a bull market, not just another bear rally. There would be no more falls that year. I immediately closed the Intel and Infineon shorts, but unfortunately kept all the other German positions, as the DAX stayed weak for another few days. As it joined the rally, I closed all the shorts there too, but still kept the options. They expired worthless.

The rally lasted throughout the year and beyond it, into 2004. The market was similar to what it had been exactly four years earlier, for the same reason: an endless flow of money poured into it. The FED kept interest rates at historic lows, though the American economy showed quite healthy signs. With this flood of money pouring into the market; the result could be nothing but a giant rally. Money feeds the stock market, like the spring feeds a river.

In early 2004, the Nasdaq broke through the 2000, the Dow the 10,000, and the DAX the 4000-point barrier. If only I had been long of DAXEX and the German stocks since I predicted the DAX would reach 4000 points! But instead, I'd sold it short several times. As is often the case, as an investor I'd had a mid-term strategy mid term, but often acted against it because of some short-term ideas. But the big money is in the big trend, just as Livermore said.

Some stocks I traded earlier reached unbelievably high prices again, at which I just missed shorting them (or was squeezed of the shorts) two years earlier. PMC-Sierra reached $25 (after bottoming at $3), Juniper $30 (bottom at $4), Broadcom $40 (bottom at $10), Veritas $40 (bottom at $10) Intel $35 and Qualcomm $60. At these prices these shares seemed sharply overvalued with a P/E well over 30 (sometimes 100), but this time I didn't short them, because the general market was so bullish and I didn't want to fight against the trend. In the case of Qualcomm, this proved to be wise: the stock was rising further throughout the year and reached $90 ($45 after the 2:1 split in August 2004).

In the case of the other stocks, it really was the top. PMC-Sierra fell in the next months below $10, Juniper, Veritas and Intel below $20. Only Broadcom stayed at about $40! The general market remained strong until early July, when the first serious correction arrived. Seeing that most of the stocks I considered overvalued had already fallen a lot, I thought the correction reaches each overvalued shares and sold Broadcom short at about $40. During the two months of the correction, it fell to $25 (I bought back at $30).

The correction was over in early September. By this time the market became pessimistic, a lot of short positions had been built up. A massive rally started, but these stocks couldn't rise again. Now the market valued them more realistically.

Google

In the last months of 2004, the bull market kicked into high gear once again. The S&P 500 broke through the giant resistance, 1165 points. The best performers were now the oil companies, but Internet shares were once again among the leaders, just like 5 years earlier. Those Internet companies which survived the crash after the bubble now started to make a profit, becoming the investors' favorites once again. First and foremost there were Yahoo, E-Bay and Amazon.

And now a new share was coming on the market, Google! The search engine company's shares were already being offered in August, when the correction of the bull market was in its sixth week, and pessimism became overwhelming. Most comments were pessimistic about the issue: many investors and analysts thought that the issue price would be the top, and they would buy on the market much lower. They were wrong...

In most cases, if expectations are so pessimistic, the price can only go up, at least for a while. I thought I would wait to see what happened on the first trading day after the issue. If the price stays above the issue price, that's a good sign for those who had bought the share, because all of them has a profit (as everyone bought at the same price) thus it isn't urgent for anyone to sell. Once the price falls below the issue price, everyone has a loss, and the triggering of stop-losses can ignite a chain reaction.

So I thought I would buy on the market and place a stop-loss a bit over the issue price. The issue price was $85; the stock opened at $95 on the first day and closed over $100. I decided to buy at $101, with a stop-loss at $95, the lowest price the share was trading the previous day. The price continued rising up to $115, then slipped back to $100. After a few days, it started rising again: a very bullish sign, because it could not fall back close to the issue price. It was surging fast: in 6 weeks it reached $150, and then after a good earnings release, the stock opened with a huge gap at $170 and continued rising. I took the 100 % profit in early November!

Surging from 100 to 200 dollars, it took only two months (see Figures 5 and 6, page 221-222), and to $300, another half year. As we can see, the easiest way up is at uncharted territory for a stock (and every other tradable instrument: currencies, commodities, bonds etc.)

The emerging miracle

As the big markets kept going up and up, emerging markets joined the rally, and as usual, they started to surge much faster. Because they are less liquid and more speculative than the developed markets, they are more volatile, offering enormous possibilities for brave traders. Most of the emerging markets reached and in some cases exceeded their year 2000 highs, while most developed market indices (Nasdaq, DAX, Footsie) were far from their earlier peaks. There may be two reasons for this: the bubble was smaller on emerging markets in 2000 (usually there weren't P/E-s over 25-30), and these markets have the potential for bigger growth (and bigger risk, of course).

The most important emerging markets are Russia, some in Asia (Thailand, Indonesia) and Latin America (Brazil, Argentina, Mexico), and the new European Union members and hopefuls in Central and Eastern Europe. Russian stocks have come a long way since the Russian crisis, and in the bull market of 2003-2005, the index rose another 100%! The price of crude oil was rising again after the toppling of Saddam, and oil is still the number one export article for Russia. The high price helped the Russian economy to grow quickly, and this of course led to rising stock prices, with oil and gas companies among the best performers.

In Latin America, the Brazilian market skyrocketed 150%, while in the same period Argentina and Mexico surged 100%. In Asia, most markets rose 50-60%, but the SET (Stock Exchange of Thailand) rose 100%, from 400 to 800 points, and the Indonesian market even more.

From 2004, European emerging markets became the leaders of the bull market, among them new EU members like the Czech Republic, Lithuania, Hungary and Poland, and the hopefuls like Romania and Bulgaria. Let's see why. These countries and their stock markets had come a long way since the period of wild capitalism. They are becoming less and less emerging and more and more developed markets, on a par with other small EU markets such as Portugal and Greece. Volatility is decreasing; short term movements in prices aren't as wild any more on these markets as they had been in the 90s.

When the strong rally became obvious, my attention turned to my old friend, the Budapest Stock Exchange. For a long time, the leader of the new bull market was OTP Bank, my favorite at the turn of the Millennia. Unfortunately, when it went to an all-time high above 3000 forints in early 2004, dragging the benchmark with it to a new high, I was on holiday and didn't follow the market. It was one of the most beautiful breakouts I have ever seen! (See Figure 7, page 223.)

By the time I got back, the share had already risen 20 percent since the breakout so I thought it would be too late to buy. It wasn't. From that level, the price doubled again, in less than a year. In this way, the share became one of the best long-term investments since it came on the market 10 years earlier, rising hundred-fold during this time. If I could have imagined it back in 1995, I would have done nothing else but bought OTP Bank for at least half of my trading capital...

So, having missed out on OTP, my attention turned to my old favorite, MOL. The former state-owned oil company became a regional multinational in Central Europe, acquiring oil refineries and gasoline stations in countries like Slovakia, Romania and Croatia. Previously, the Hungarian state had forced the company to subsidize the price of natural gas for non-industrial consumers, so the losses of the natural gas subsidiary ate up most of the profit of the oil subsidiary. For this reason, the share didn't take part in the 1999-2000 bull market at all. Its price remained at about 5000 forints ($20) for many years.

In 2003, the situation changed. Oil prices started skyrocketing, and the gap between the price of crude oil and refined products widened, increasing profits for refineries. From 2004, MOL stopped subsidizing natural gas prices so the natural gas subsidiary itself became profit-making. In November 2003, still before this was announced, the share price surged sharply. When there were rumors about the announcement, many traders, myself included, bought a lot of shares between 6500 and 7000 forints. After the announcement, the price started falling, and kept slipping for about 2 months. It was a *fait accompli*, or the case of 'buy on rumor, sell on news'.

As the price didn't stop falling and I had a lot of shares, I triggered a stop-loss at 6500 forints. The price slipped even further: the bottom was a bit under 6000.

Bull market again

Although the share then started rising again, this time I didn't buy it until it reached an *all-time high* 3 months later, over 7200 forints. If a stock rises to uncharted territory and doesn't immediately fall back, it's often one of the best times to buy it! Many people will think it's expensive, just because the price is higher than ever, but in most cases, this isn't true. Think it over: at a new high nobody has a loss on the stock; nobody is forced to sell. On the contrary, all those who don't have the share, feel the pressure to jump on the bandwagon. And when an investor buys at the all-time high, it is very easy to set up the stop-loss: at the level of the former top. A good stock can retest that level, but never breaks it.

So I bought MOL at the all-time high, about 7300 forints and set up a target price of 15,000 forints. My colleagues thought I was crazy: they said they couldn't imagine a price much over 10,000. In a year it was 20,000 ($100)! That's how MOL became the one and only share I was able to make money on in every bull market since the company went public in 1994, on its long way from 600 forints.

At the same time, the benchmark index of the market went to an all-time high at 10,800 points. It slowly rose further to 12,000, but then in a year's time it soared to over 20,000. As funds and individual investors all over the world discovered that emerging markets and especially Central and Eastern European ones had been rising fast, they all wanted to join and rushed to buy into these markets, accelerating the trend themselves.

Forint and bonds

After so many years, the Hungarian currency once again became an interesting speculative tool. In 2001 the devaluation on a continuous basis was finally over and the forint was pegged to the euro, but at the same time, it could move in a range of 15 percent both ways; once it strengthens or weakens to the edge of this band, the National Bank of Hungary intervenes. The National Bank kept the forint interest rates relatively high, at about 8-10%, to attract foreign capital, and thus strengthen the forint temporarily, to lower inflation.

From the first moment, the forint was gradually rising. As interest rates in Europe and the US were cut several times, the rate difference between the forint and the big currencies widened to 7-8 percent. This attracted further capital to the country and the forint rallied further. In early 2003, it got close to the edge of the band; it had only a few more percent to go up, but almost 30% downside. I didn't really understand those who still kept buying it.

It wasn't longer before I learned why people were still buying forints: rumors were spreading that the band in which the forint could move would be widened so the forint could strengthen further against the euro. Many investors, among them large funds, started to speculate on this, buying enormous sums of forints, pushing the price to the edge, and forcing the National Bank to buy euros. They thought they could force the

Bank to give up the band and let the forint float so that it could surge further.

The Bank bought €5 billion in 2 days! Just to show what an enormous sum it is for such a small country, prior to this Hungary's currency reserves had been just €10 billion. At the same time, it lowered interest rates sharply, so the difference between the forint and euro rates wasn't so huge any more. When investors saw that there would be no band widening, they started profit taking, and the forint dropped 5% in one day.

But what could those investors who had sold billions of euros just a day earlier do? And who were they? They must have been big hedge funds; nobody else has such a huge sum of money for such purposes. They hoped they could force the widening.

The question arises: how could they be this silly? Usually funds speculate against a currency when it is weak and should be devalued but a central bank or government doesn't let it fall. In this case the central bank sells dollars or euros as long as it has them, but when it runs out, they are forced to devalue, as has been seen in so many countries.

But nobody ever tried to force a currency to appreciate! They should have known that a central bank could sell as much as it likes of its own money so buy any amount of foreign currency without any move in the exchange rate. I can't imagine where these funds got such a ludicrous idea, but ultimately they lost a huge sum, about 5% of €5 billion, or €250 million. The winner of course was the National Bank of Hungary,which soon sold the cheaply-bought euros 5% higher, stabilizing the rate there for a time.

And that wasn't still the end. The rate was stable for two months, but then the forint suddenly fell another 10%. All the remaining euro-shorts (forint-longs) were squeezed. The market seemed to find the balance here, where it had been before the band widening. But this time, the National Bank considered the exchange rate to low and raised interests rates to 12.5% just to strengthen the forint this time. I think it was a mistake; the state had to pay this huge interest rate on treasury bonds. It is a burden for the budget and thus the taxpayers.

With such forint rates (10-percentage points over euro and dollar rates), buying Hungarian bonds was worthwhile, just as I had found 18 years earlier. The interest rate had been then quite high without a good reason, and now the situation was the same. Isn't it funny how history repeats itself, even in a trader's life?

This interesting speculating opportunity, and the forint itself, will soon be over. It has to find a more or less equilibrium exchange rate against the euro and stabilize there before it will be simply replaced by it, as Hungary joins the European currency union.

Compensation notes again

In 2003, there was once again a good deal with an old favorite of mine, the compensation note. Some 12 years

Bull market again

after its release, it still existed. The Hungarian state still hadn't provided enough shares of privatized companies for the whole amount of notes that had been issued; there were still about 5% of the original quantity of notes on the market. The market price was 700 forints, or 70% of the face value.

After the elections in 2002, the new government decided to solve the problem of the remaining notes. It founded a company holding state-owned shares and real estate and announced plans to issue the shares of the holding company for the compensation notes. The price of the note started to rise. When I heard that a group of investors plan to get the majority in the holding company and that they were collecting the notes for this, I decided to buy at 900 forints. In a few months, I sold at over 1300, taking a nearly 50% profit. And what a good decision! After the issue, the price of the holding company fell to 800 forints; the remaining notes fell to 500. Why? Nobody knew. There were hardly any notes left outstanding. Maybe some note holders thought there would be no more occasions to use their notes and dumped them.

For the speculators, it provided a good opportunity again. In early 2004, the price started rising steeply and more than doubled in a few months' time. There were rumors that the state would sell another stake in the holding company that had been partly privatized in the previous year, or would pay cash for the remaining notes. There remained sow few notes outstanding on the market that any rumor could ignite a huge rally.

As it turned out, the last state-owned companies were privatized, and buyers were allowed to pay with notes. This way, the price once again rose to 1300 forints, and virtually all the remaining notes disappeared from the market, as even the most desperate holders sold at this price. After so many years, the good old compensation note was still worth speculating for...

And in the meantime, we found another similar kind of compensation note, issued in Bulgaria!, It was listed on the Sofia Stock Exchange and trading between 20 and 25 percent of the face value (or 20-25 levas, the Bulgarian currency).

Well, my Bulgarian friend and I thought we should consider buying it at this level. From our experience with the Hungarian compensation notes we knew that this price was very attractive. So at the end of 2003 we bought at about 22-23 levas for our fund investing in Bulgaria and as private investors as well.

For almost a year nothing happened, but then one day the price of the note started to rise sharply with heavy volume. It broke through the earlier top of 26 levas and kept rising. Rumors started to circulate that a long-awaited transaction was imminent: the state would sell shares of the Bulgarian Telecom Company for compensation notes. The rumor proved to be true: shortly it was announced that 35% of the Company's shares were available for the notes. The price of the note soon surged to well over 100 levas, and after the initial public offer, the price of Bulgarian Telecom doubled within 6 months.

Oil vs. dollar

Still before the Iraq war, the market expected the price of crude oil to fall back to $20 a barrel or even lower, once the war was over. But it didn't. On the contrary, after a fast drop, it started rising again and kept rising throughout 2003 and beyond. Although the exploration was increasing, the demand was increasing faster.

Until the nineties the main consumers of crude oil were the developed regions: Europe, the US, Japan, and some other countries. The population of these regions represented less than one fourth of the world population. In the late nineties China started to join the industrialized nations with a staggering 10 percent economic growth a year. The growing industry needed more energy, and at the same time, as their income was increasing, people started to use cars, computers and electronic devices just like elsewhere in the developed world, consuming more and more gasoline and electricity. But the Chinese population is as big as that of the former developed world altogether! It is a giant demand for energy, first of all crude oil.

In 2004, the trend continued and the price broke through $40, its top of 14 years earlier, and went to an all-time high. The surge continued to $55, but then a sharp correction pushed the price back to $40. I thought that this strong barrier, which now acted as a support, couldn't be broken. I decided, for the first time in my life, to speculate on crude oil and opened some long futures (in other words, I bought oil). It was a wise decision: the price surged to a new high within 3 months.

On a par with crude oil, the prices of oil companies themselves were rising, and they became the leaders of the bull market among stocks. Their earnings increased fast as oil refining became more and more profitable, due to an increasing shortage of refining capacities. That's how Exxon became the biggest-cap company in the world, overtaking General Electric and Microsoft. Some oil companies on emerging markets surged even faster, among them my long time favorite, MOL.

Other commodities like gold, copper and others also got to a bull trend on a par with crude oil. But here we should notice something interesting: the price of all these commodities was rising only in dollar terms (and of course in currencies tied to the US dollar) for long. In a lot of other currencies, the rise was not so sharp. In euro terms, the price of crude oil didn't even reach a new high, while in dollar terms it rose more than 40% above the former top! So energy prices were rising sharply in the US while only slightly in the eurozone. How was this possible?

The answer is the weakening of the dollar against other currencies, first of all the euro and the yen since the year 2000. The main reasons for this were historic lows in US interest rates, a record deficit in US trade and the increasing acceptance of the euro as an equal currency for the dollar, prompting central banks to increase the share of the euro in their currency reserves.

In 2004-2005, the FED raised rates several times, making them higher than those of the euro-zone, and this way preventing the further weakening of the US currency. Oil prices continued rising, this way they reached an all-time high in euro terms as well. In the longer term, I expect the two currencies to return to parity.

Where the sun never sets

As 2005 was approaching, I studied the stock market conditions carefully and found that the US market had become overvalued, and thought this couldn't last long while American interest rates and oil prices were rising. The situation started to remind me of the end of the 1972 bull market, which was followed by the famous bear of 1973-74, the time of the first oil crisis. I decided to buy put options for some stocks and index-related instruments, such as DIA, QQQQ, SPY and SMH (Semiconductor Holders Trust)

In the first days of 2005, the market tumbled, as I expected, and this continued for the whole of January. The S&P 500 fell back to the former resistance, 1165 points, which now behaved as a strong support. As I didn't expect it to break the support for the first time, I took the profits on the options and waited. I was planning to buy them again after a rally, but in the next month prices once again rose too sharply; the S&P 500 even exceeded its previous high!

Adventurous moneymaking

All the markets reached their peak on March 9, exactly 5 years after the top of the tech bubble, and in the next days, they fell sharply. But once again only temporarily: the bull market went on, especially in Europe. The DAX and the Footsie reached soon new four-year highs, not to mention the smaller Central European markets and Russia

In the summer, I had the pleasure of visiting the Bovespa, the Stock Exchange in Sao Paulo. It was like the Budapest market 8-10 years earlier: the visitors' gallery was full of excited investors and speculators. They traded, followed prices, talked to each other and had a wonderful time.

After the closing bell, I started thinking: in one hour, Wall Street is closing too. And then trading is just beginning in Australia, and in a few hours, markets are opening in Tokyo, Bangkok and Delhi. And when they close, European markets are just opening. And when it's afternoon in London and Frankfurt, trading is beginning again in Sao Paulo and then Wall Street...

As Kostolany says: the sun never sets on the stock exchange!

PART TWO:

Stories of other investors from the time of transition

These are the stories of six different people I know who tried to make money in the turbulent times of the transition from communism to a free market economy: The Bond Trader, The Journalist, The Privatizer, The 'Greedy', The Disciplined Trader, and The Gambler Genius. Some of them had already started during the last years of communism, while others, mostly the younger ones, started a bit later, when privatization kicked into high gear and Central and Eastern Europe started to join the developed world economically. Some of them got rich, others only managed to make a good living, and one went bankrupt; half of them moved on and continued trading on the world stock markets. The stories are all interesting, each offering a different perspective on this unprecedented and exciting period.

1. THE BOND TRADER

The Bond Trader is a good friend of mine. Around the time when he became a university student, years before me, the first bonds were issued in Hungary. His attention, just as mine, was caught by the incredibly high interest rates paid on these bonds. He would even have stood in queues to buy them – if he had had any money. But he didn't have a penny. However, he did have something else that he thought might be valuable. It was an old, beautiful piece of furniture, a table. He didn't know exactly what it was worth, but he hoped to get enough for it to start trading. He called an expert to value the table, and to his surprise, the expert identified it as a very famous desk that used to belong to Queen Elizabeth, wife of Austrian Emperor and Hungarian King Franz Joseph. How did this piece of furniture get to my friend's house?

The Queen had kept this desk (as well as other furniture) at her favorite place, in one of the emperor's palaces not far from Budapest. In 1918, at the end of World War I, the Austro-Hungarian monarchy broke apart into numerous small countries. In Hungary, complete turmoil and lawlessness followed the war. There were no borders and different armies occupied different parts of the country. In the central region, a short-lived communist government took over in 1919. During this period, looting was common, especially in 'bourgeois' places like Franz Joseph's former palace. The monarchy was gone and the property of the Habsburgs had been left unguarded. Somebody took the table and later gave it to my friend's grandfather, who was a high school teacher. He took it to the school where he worked and when he retired a few decades later, the school gave it back to him as a present; he in turn gave it to his grandson before he died.

Now the Bond Trader sold the table to a museum. This way he had some money and could buy his first bonds. He was surprised to see that some bonds with the same interest rates were being sold at a higher price than others, just because the name of the issuing company sounded better. He decided to buy the cheaper ones with the higher yield.

Carefully watching the new issues, he saw that every now and then there would be a new bond with a better yield, so he started to exchange his bonds.

After awhile, he found a very special one, issued by a telephone company. At that time, like many other products and services in communist countries, there was a lack of telephone landlines. But if the people who were waiting for a line bought these bonds, they had a chance of getting a line sooner, so people bought the bonds at face value and when they received their phone line, sold them at the much lower market price. The loss on the bonds was seen as part of the cost of

The Bond Trader

getting a telephone line. The Bond Trader bought these special bonds with a yield of 15% or sometimes more (nobody else bought them with an expiry of 12 years).

When he realized what a good profit he could make from year to year, he suggested to his family and some friends that he handles their money, offering them an 8% return (compared to just 3-5% in the banks) while making 15-20% himself.

Later, when more banks were buying and selling bonds, a new opportunity arose. Inflation and interest rates had gone up but the interest rate paid by the bonds remained the same, so the return was not as huge as before. The banks this time tried to trade at unrealistic prices. There was a huge gap between their buying and selling prices, so the Bond Trader could easily buy above their bid and sell under their offer in front of the banks and still turn a good profit.

A bit later, an even bigger profit was available due to the craziness of the banks. One bank would sell a bond for 102 percent of the face value while another one bought the same bond for 104! The Bond Trader bought at 102 and sold at 104 until the first bank ran out of the bonds. Is there a better and easier arbitrage opportunity? And how could such a thing happen?

The answer is simple: the banks, after 40 years of communism, were still inexperienced. When the rate of inflation exceeded the interest rate of the bonds, the price of the bonds fell below their face value. The banks simply didn't want to see lower prices because they feared people wouldn't trust the bond market, so they started subsidizing the bond prices when they bought from the small holders and selling in bulk to another bank with a loss, hoping that the situation wouldn't last too long.

This way the second bank had a lot of bonds and tried to sell a bit higher than it bought, but still lower than the price the first bank offered. The Bond Trader was rushing to the second bank to buy big quantities at the lower price, and then bringing the bonds to the first bank in small quantities, as a small holder, making a nice profit for himself in the process.

As inflation kept rising further, the issuing companies started to grant a premium interest rate for their bonds. In some cases it was 5% or more, so the price of the bond jumped immediately. The Bond Trader would try to guess which bond would be next: he bought the bond and waited for the announcement. In some cases, he called the company on the phone posing as a small investor and asked them if they were planning to pay a premium. If they said 'yes, we are taking it into consideration', he bought the bond and waited for the almost sure extra payment.

When the Stock Exchange re-opened, he considered buying the issue of the first listed stock, but decided to just sit on a bond and wait for the anticipated 5-10% premium instead. He wasn't willing to trade the certainty of a 5-10% profit for the uncertainty of the stock market and that has remained his principle, to have a small but more secure profit in bonds rather than go for the bigger but riskier profits on the stock market.

The Bond Trader

2 years later, the Bond Trader started trading compensation notes, just like I did. By this time, he had a lot of capital saved so he didn't bother buying from the small holders. He rather bought in bulk from traders like me, at higher prices. When it became possible to exchange the notes for IBUSZ shares, he exchanged about one-fourth of all the available shares!

It was around this time that we first met, in the new building of the Stock Exchange. I sold him my notes; I had still relatively little cash so I had to sell every day in order to have enough money to buy more notes. So I bought and sold, and my friend exchanged the notes for shares, making a much bigger profit.

There were about ten more note-to-share offerings in the next two years. With so many notes, he was able to get in every time, even when there were new issues and there was a certain risk (unlike in the case of IBUSZ, which was quoted at a higher price on the Stock Exchange). Unlike most note-speculators, he took these risks, and usually they were worth it. In some cases, the price of the new issues fell on the market, but in most cases a strong demand emerged for them, causing a strong rally in their prices.

Just like me, the Bond Trader built a network of compensation-note agents throughout the country. Twice a week he traveled around and collected the notes. When he had more than could be exchanged for shares, he sold the surplus to brokerage companies. We often worked together, offering our packets jointly in order to get a better price for the bigger quantity.

Adventurous moneymaking

When the compensation note period wound down, he started trading treasury bonds. When inflation surged and bonds were depressed, he bought long-term bonds, expecting inflation and yields to fall and the price of bonds to rise sharply, and he was right again.

The Bond Trader rarely invests in stocks, saying they are too risky, and he thinks that futures and anything else on margin are evil. He mainly trades bonds and bond-related investment funds; he is on of the biggest bond experts I know.

2. THE JOURNALIST

The Journalist chose his parents' profession and went into journalism. But even as a teenager, he was already interested in much more things: mathematics, statistics and above all money. To be more precise, he wanted to have the latter.

When the first bonds were issued, he was working for an economics magazine. He started to write about the bonds and learned everything he could about them in a very short time, meeting anybody and writing about anything with a connection to bonds. After a while he naturally began to see all the possibilities that the Bond Trader had seen. He had been working for a few years and had saved up some money. Using this sum he did the same as the Bond Trader, but with a difference: he was sitting in the editorial office, and those who wanted to buy or sell bonds simply called him. That was how I met him: I called the magazine he worked for, talked to him, and sold him my bonds.

Thus he himself became an institution, the market instead of the market. Many people were interested in buying or selling bonds: they either found the Bond Trader in front of the bank or called the Journalist, the only expert at one of the two economic magazines in the country.

In the two years leading up to the re-opening of the Stock Exchange, 'exchange days' were held for those who wanted to buy or sell bonds. This functioned like a real exchange but without brokers; anyone could enter and take part. The Journalist was there every time, first just to report about it in his magazine, later as one of the biggest traders. He met the Bond Trader there, and from that time they often worked together, exchanging information, going to 'arbitrate' the banks when one was selling a bond at a lower price than another one was buying at, or simply buying bonds with incredible yields.

On the stock market, his main advantage was his connections. He rushed to introduce himself to every possible participant in the small, fledgling Hungarian market, from the issuers to the newly founded brokerage companies. This way he always got the necessary information in time.

The Journalist was ready to buy some stocks on the OTC market that almost nobody else bought, at low prices. These were the stocks of companies that hadn't been privatized yet: only a few percent of their shares were available. These stocks were later issued and listed on the Stock Exchange.

At the same time, he specialized in shares that were never listed on the Exchange. He bought these shares and when he had acquired a large amount, he offered his package to the company itself. As a journalist he could approach the management of these companies, so he knew whom to offer the shares to. The management could then ask the main owners of the company, and if they were interested, he would promise to sell them a certain amount of shares at a certain price. For a big package, they were ready to offer a substantially higher price.

Before the Russian crisis, he did buy some shares on the Stock Exchange because he thought they were a good deal but he made a loss on these shares, and as he needed the cash for his OTC deals, he sold them with loss rather than keeping them and waiting for the recovery.

Later, the Jounalist made a truly wonderful trade. A certain company, listed on the Stock Exchange, sold 830,000 of its shares at an auction using the book building method, which means that prospective buyers placed their bids for as many shares as they wanted, at whatever price they were ready to pay. The buyer with the highest bid received his shares, and then the next highest bid received his, and so on until all the shares had been sold. This meant that buyers could get their stocks at different prices, with the highest price potentially being double or even triple that of the lowest. The Journalist developed a theory about the weakness of this system and placed his bids at many price levels like a pyramid.

The market price was 150 forints, but after the news of the auction there were no buyers on the Exchange. He placed bids at 130 forints for 2000 shares, at 120 forints for 6000 shares, at 105 for 18,000 shares, and so on all the way down, for bigger and bigger quantities.

Adventurous moneymaking

At 23 forints, he was ready to buy the whole package. He reasoned that by using this method no matter what price he got his shares at, his average price would be less than that of the other buyers. The Journalist was right: he bought 540,000 shares at an average price of 31 forints (his lowest price being 200,000 shares at 23 forints each), while the remaining 270,000 shares were bought by others for an average price of 55 forints. This way he bought two-third of the whole package, about 40% cheaper than the others!

After the auction, the price on the Stock Exchange was 55 forints and in two weeks' time it had risen to 100 forints, as the market saw that there wasn't any extra selling pressure after the auction. The Journalist sold all of his shares at 92 forints, making a staggering 200 percent profit in just two weeks! But it's important to remember that he needed a huge amount of cash for this deal as he had to be ready to buy the whole package of shares at the auction.

On the main European and American markets, he decided to trade options rather than shares. In October 2002, he bought call options for some German and American stocks with an expiration date in January 2005: a year later he had made enormous profits on them. The nicest was a QQQQ call option with an expiry in 2005 January and a strike price at $20, which he bought for $6 and sold a year later for $15.

Finally with the Privatizer (see on page 170) and another investor the Journalist bought the majority of shares in the Budapest Stock Exchange itself! And a bit later, the Commodity Exchange too. They were planning to unify the two markets, thus re-creating a joint Budapest Stock and Commodity Exchange, but some Austrian banks and the Vienna Stock Exchange placed such a good bid for their shares that they couldn't resist the temptation and sold them.

Could it be a greater success in the life of a speculator, than buying the Stock Exchange itself?

3. THE PRIVATIZER

As others had before them, three young guys, among them the Privatizer realized what a good opportunity the compensation note business was in 1995. They had an excellent idea: to exploit the huge difference between the market price and the face value of the compensation note in bulk when the price (20% the of face value) was so low that virtually nobody was selling.

There had been no shares offered for the notes for awhile so they couldn't be used for anything. But the Privatizer knew that it was just a matter of time so they created a kind of investment fund and offered shares in this fund to note holders. They promised them that with their collected notes, the fund would be able to participate in privatization, and if successful, it would pay a nice dividend on the shares. The note holders liked the idea, figuring they had nothing to lose; they could either exchange their notes for shares in this unproven fund or sell them at 20%. Some of them considered it a great business opportunity: they couldn't see any difference between the shares of the best companies sold by the state and the shares of this fund containing only compensation notes and promises. The Privatizer and his friends were satisfied.

The demand for their shares was so huge that the three friends soon decided to start two more funds and offer shares in them for notes as well. All the shares of these funds were sold, but they had to advertise aggressively. At first they were in an awkward position because they didn't have the capital for this purpose, so they started to dump the collected notes to raise enough cash to pay for advertising, keeping about half of the notes in the fund to exchange for shares in privatized companies.

At the privatization auctions, they could pay with the notes, which were worth their face value plus the interest rate paid by the state earlier, or 174% of the face value altogether. With the market value of the notes at just 20%, which was only 12% of the 'official' value, in real terms they were only paying about 12% for the state property.

The Privatizer managed the most successful fund. He sold preferred shares to the note holders and kept the voting shares for himself. The small holders didn't care; they didn't want to go to annual meetings and vote, they were just hoping for a nice dividend later.

The fund's first investment was a hotel chain being sold by the state at a reasonable price, but as I mentioned, it cost the Privatizer only a fraction (10-15%) of the this price by paying with the notes. After the deal, he sold the best hotel in the chain for cash and the price he got for it was more than the market value of the notes he had paid for the whole chain! Practically, the remaining hotel chain cost him nothing...

His second privatization deal involved buying a state-owned holding company. Once again the Privatizer paid for it with compensation notes and integrated it into his fund. From this point on, the fund itself became a holding company. His third deal using compensation notes was another hotel chain, this time one that contained the former state trade union guesthouses. By controlling these two hotel chains he had a monopoly over budget accommodation, which produced not only a nice profit but also the cash flow the Privatizer needed in order to acquire more companies without relying on compensation notes.

His next step was to buy wholesale and retail pharmacy chains from the state and from local councils. He merged these chains and sold the unified company to a German buyer, turning a big profit in the process.

By this time, the Privatizer was paying dividends to his shareholders, and at the same time, offering them to buy back the shares. The former compensation note holders sold sooner or later, happy to get a better return than they would have received for their notes two years earlier. In this way he gradually became almost the sole owner of the giant holding company.

His company was growing and there was so much cash in it that the Privatizer decided to buy whole companies that he thought were bargains on the Stock Exchange. In other words, he placed takeover bids. He would then reorganize the company, sell some of its valuable real estate, and finally sell the company on with a nice profit.

Companies taken over by the Privatizer included the chain of formerly state-owned secondhand shops, a building materials producer and several companies in the meat industry, among them salami makers.

And at the end he and the Journalist with another guy bought the exchanges themselves, and sold with a huge profit to the Austrian banks.

4. THE 'GREEDY'

In the first days of capitalism in 1990, the 'Greedy' decided to try his luck as an entrepreneur in Budapest. With a friend, he set up a local cable television company and five years later they sold it with a nice profit. The 'Greedy' invested the money in treasury bonds.

Like so many others, he was drawn to the Stock Exchange by the bull market of 1996-97. Seeing the ever-rising prices, he joined the herd of buyers. First – at the suggestion of his broker – he bought some particular small-cap shares. These didn't perform as well as other investments might have, but the bull was running so he decided to open index futures positions and this way in January 1997 he doubled his money.

During the Asian Contagion he lost some of his profit, but next year, when a right-wing government won the first round of elections in a surprise result (the market considered it rather bad because a radical party took part in the coalition), he immediately sold short and turned an enormous profit on the very first day.

I met him on the Stock Exchange when he tried to sell me his old mobile phone and from that day on we spent lots of time talking about the market. Later, when Russia defaulted, we sold some stocks short together.

The 'Greedy'

At first everything was all right, but we didn't cover in time. During the furious, after-crisis rally, I was able to change my position, which saved me. The Greedy was stubborn and his money was gone.

It took him a year to get some fresh money. He recognized the pre-Y2K rally before any of us, all the way back in October 1999. He opened 50 contracts of long BUX index futures. In December, he had such a profit that he had sufficient collateral to open another 50. According to his original plan, these 100 contracts were what he had planned to open altogether; he intended to sit on them as long as the bull was running. He was the most optimistic of all of us, expecting the benchmark to reach 20,000 points in a year. At that time it was just less than 10,000 points but in January 2000, it broke through 10,000 and it was at that point that he became really greedy.

Using his new profit as collateral, he opened another 100 contracts. I jokingly told him, 'You'll feed it up to 500 contracts, get rich and then lose everything in the first pullback.' I was right, although he had only 300 contracts when it happened. The bull market was soon over, earlier than anyone had expected. The BUX index peaked at 10,700 points before turning south. Had the 'Greedy' kept only the original 100 contracts, he could have closed them when the index fell back under 10,000 with a decent profit.

His money was gone; he had no choice but to stop trading. Instead, he founded the Association of Small Investors. He has been President of this organization since then, quite successfully.

In 2004, history repeated itself. The one year old bull on the emerging markets drew the 'Greedy' to the Stock Exchange again. By this time, he had been able to save up a sum suitable for trading again. When the market reached an all-time high, he opened 10 contracts of long index futures.

He said once again that he was not planning to buy more. But as the market soared further, the 'Greedy' couldn't resist the temptation, bought more and more, just like in old long times. He had 25 contracts when the first correction arrived. The market went to a wild ride, and this time he could control the situation: he closed his positions just in time, without loss. Maybe one day he will be a good trader, after getting rid of his greediness...

5. THE DISCIPLINED TRADER

After finishing high school, the Disciplined Trader went to Finland to learn languages and work for a year. He was able to save enough money to start investing back in Hungary. When he returned and started university, he invested the money in treasury bonds. Like the Bond Trader, he always searched out those with a high yield.

In 1995, when inflation and interest rates peaked and started dropping fast, he bought a special bond, which paid an interest rate tied to the inflation of the previous year plus a 3 percent premium. As inflation fell sharply, the yield of these bonds was high in real terms, generating a nice profit for the him.

Next year, the falling interest rates and skyrocketing share prices drew the Disciplined Trader to the Stock Exchange. The first stock he bought was MOL – his broker suggested it – but the share immediately fell while others surged so he stopped listening to brokers. He started to trade futures, opening mainly long positions, and made profit most of the time.

Up to this point, his story is similar to that of the 'Greedy', but the difference is that the Disciplined Trader has been trading since then with success. His secret lies in his strict self-control. He only opens relatively small positions and uses the stop-loss rigorously. In this way his profits are limited but unlike most traders, he is continuously making a profit.

I remember once he opened two or three contracts of BUX futures and we were laughing at him, but he was right. He never risked more than a few percent of his capital in one trade, so his losses always remained under control, while most of his trades were successful, or if not, the profit on the winning trades was much more than the loss on the losing ones.

At the Stock Exchange he met the Journalist, who asked him to write articles for the same economic daily I was writing for; the Disciplined Trader has been a journalist and stock market expert ever since.

During the Russian crisis he was heavily short (like me) and closed the shorts at the right time (unlike me), and then opened long positions after Greenspan saved the world (like me again). He made quite nice money during and after the Russian turmoil!

Since 2001 the Disciplined Trader has been trading on the big European and American markets. His first stock on them was Nokia, which he bought at exactly the same time as I did, before the expected warning in March 2001; although we had the same position, we didn't realize it at the time.

His second share was KPN. As he was watching CNBC, he saw the Dutch telecom share tumbling and then suddenly turning. He bought it at €5 and sold at €7 in a few days' time and from then on he always tried to catch the turnaround stories. If a share fell a lot but seemed about to turn, he bought into it with a rigorous stop-loss.

He always uses a stop-loss except when he buys a penny share; with penny shares he is prepared to lose all the money he has invested, like a premium for an option. Using this method he made his biggest gain in percentage terms with Worldcom. As the share fell to almost zero amid bankruptcy rumors, he bought it at 5 cents. What was the risk? It was just four ticks from the lowest possible price... And after the bankruptcy became fact, the share started surging (fait accompli). He sold it at 18 cents, just one trading day after he bought it at 5 cents!

The Disciplined Trader prefers the small, less liquid shares that stand at very low prices, so any movement in their price is large in percentage terms. He found lots of such penny shares on the emerging markets and made nice profits with them. After a while, he started hunting for such stocks on the Nasdaq.

Every day after market hours, he searches for stocks under $2 that are among the price percentage gainers. If it was the first such winning day for one, he is buying it still in the opening the next day. In most cases these stocks rise further; if not, he is dumping them. He only buys when he considers the general trend bullish because he doesn't like to fight the trend.

In 2003, he bought SINA and made a huge profit with it. He had another Chinese favorite, DFCT, which he bought several times at 30-40 cents and sold at 50-60 cents. He also picked up the stocks of security and protection equipment maker companies, when these became mania stocks in 2004; among others IPIX and Abatix corp. These shares had been trading at about $3, when the investors suddenly discovered them. The Disciplined Trader bought into them after the first rising day with big volume; and sold them within a few days with a profit of more than 100%!

How could these stocks surge so sharply? The answer is simple: investors from the whole world were searching for such stocks after a year of bull market. The daily volume of such a share was sometimes 10-20 times the capital stock of the company! So many investors and so few shares at the same time; the result of course is skyrocketing. And when this mania was over, the hordes of traders dumped the same shares, and the price fell to its fraction within a few days.

The Disciplined Trader also has another specialty, a strategy for trading before earnings releases. If a share is overbought before the earnings release and analysts are expecting a very good result, he sells the share short right before the earnings release, expecting the case of 'fait accompli'. He often buys the same stock in the next quarter, when the public is already disappointed and expectations are pessimistic, so the earnings can be a pleasant surprise.

He never buys a share for more than $5000; he is simply unwilling to take such a risk, with the exception of index-related stocks, where the risk is substantially smaller.

6. THE GAMBLER GENIUS

I've already mentioned the Gambler Genius; he's the trader who made the ingenious trade with the two million Marconi shares.

I first met him in 1994 when he came into my office to buy compensation notes to exchange for stocks. He was working in a bank and later for brokerage houses when he started trading stocks and futures on the Budapest Stock Exchange.

As his capital grew, the Gambler Genius opened bigger and bigger positions. He made his first really big killing in the Russian crisis; on the day when a brokerage house sold index futures 20% under the market price, he bought more than 300 contracts (I bought 40) and made $100,000!

In October 1999, he had a long position worth 1.5 billion forints (more than $5 million) on a margin of about $1 million, which raises the question of why the brokerage house let him trade with a margin of 1:5. The answer is the same as in the case of Livermore almost 100 years earlier: the brokerage house wanted the huge commission and they knew if he went bankrupt, he could always start over and work his way back up to trading giant quantities yet again.

Now the market plummeted and the Gambler Genius was losing heavily. His margin fell from $1 million to about 200,000. Then, at the market bottom, two-third of his 5-million position was liquidated, but the late 1999 rally was so huge that the remaining positions covered the entire $800,000 loss on the way up!

He started trading on the Nasdaq in early 2001. In the Easter rally, he bought and sold shares without significant profits or losses; he was just learning about trading on this much more liquid and volatile market. Once he had 80,000 shares of Intel in a day trade!

In August that year, as the market was tumbling, the Gambler Genius started buying into the falling knives. He bought Ciena at about $13, Juniper at $15, thirty thousand shares each. Prices fell further, and on 9/11, the market was suspended.

When it reopened a week later, the two stocks fell like stones. At the bottom, Ciena was at about $9, Juniper about $10. If they had fallen another $1.50, his margin would have gone to zero but the brokerage company decided not to liquidate, for two reasons. First, the brokers considered the market so oversold that that they saw a good chance for a rebound. Second, these stocks were so liquid (with a volume of 30 million a day) that this quantity, thirty thousand shares, could be sold anytime within a 30-40 cent range, so it would be enough to start liquidation if the stock fell another dollar.

This way the Gambler Genius was able to avoid liquidation and survive the bottom, and the furious

'Taliban rally' saved him. When the stocks surged to about $15-16, he sold them with a small profit. That same day after the market close, Juniper jumped to $20 with a gap; he should have waited one more day to close this position that had almost ruined him with a big profit..

Next summer, when stock markets simply couldn't find bottom, the Gambler Genius bought into Verisign on its way down at $20. He expected an upside correction that never came. Instead of triggering a stop-loss, he was waiting and hoping each day, until the price finally crashed. He dumped the shares after the gap, at $11 (see Figure 11, page 254). It was a huge package, thirty thousand shares. His loss was $270,000 on this trade alone.

I'll mention just two more of his trades; these are both beautiful. The first one he made with Qualcomm when it was tumbling faster and faster after staying well over $50. When it plummeted to almost $30 and the line of least resistance seemed to turn upward, the Gambler Genius decided to buy 50,000 shares at $31. He recognized the moment when the stock was extremely oversold and a fast correction was just beginning. He sold it on the same day at $35 and made $200,000 with this quick day trade!

His other amazing trade took place in the summer of 2002 when after the five-month relentless fall the market was finally turning. The day it happened was such a perfect bottom day; it was easy to recognize (I bought Nokia and Microsoft that day). The Gambler

Genius bought 30,000 shares of Microsoft at $41.50 and sold a few hours later at $46!

He has ingenious ideas from time to time but as soon as he makes a huge profit he starts gambling. When the next position shows a loss, he behaves like a sucker: he doesn't use a stop-loss or profit lock-in. And when he is almost bankrupt, he starts acting as a brilliant trader again. This way his worth is constantly fluctuating between zero and $1 million. We tried to stop him when he had the million, but it was impossible; he was blinded by the promise of wealth. It's a constant cycle: when he has nothing he is a genius, but when he makes his fortune, he is becoming a gambler.

PART THREE:

A beginner's guide to the stock market

1. WHY DO WE NEED THE STOCK EXCHANGE AND HOW IT WORKS

Many people I meet ask me what the stock exchange is for. The answer is simple: the stock market is the place where companies can easily collect capital for future development. Those who are ready to give money to a company by buying shares at a public offering can take part in its success (or possibly its failure, of course) without actually working for the company.

As an example, imagine young Bill Gates or Hewlett and Packard trying to convince a bank to back their seemingly far-fetched plans for electronics, PCs, software etc. The bank considers the risk too big and turns them down, leaving Microsoft and Hewlett-Packard no choice but to turn to the stock exchange. They issue shares and those investors ready to take part in these enterprises, unlike the banks, buy the shares.

In this way, the companies could raise the necessary capital to make their ideas reality, and in this case, the investors who took part made an incredible profit on their investment; a one-dollar investment in Microsoft in 1986 was worth more than $350 fifteen years later. Of course, there are enterprises that fail, but almost all of the successful ones collected capital on the stock market. All the industrial development of the past two to three hundred years would have been impossible without this concentration of capital, and that would have been impossible without the stock market.

Once the stocks are issued, investors want to be sure that they can sell their stocks and can buy them again, or can decide to invest in other companies. The stock exchange allows anyone to buy and sell their shares at any time. That market is more effective if greater quantities can be bought or sold, without a big move in the price.

On the stock market, there are different participants, including institutions such as mutual, pension and hedge funds, investment banks, and insurance companies, as well as private investors. There are investors who buy for mid or long term, say one year or more, and there are short-term investors, or rather speculators, who speculate in search of fast movements. They not only buy shares; they also sell them short if they expect a falling period. Finally there are the day traders who open a position (long or short) but close it within the same trading day. The short-term speculative traders and day traders are very important for the market because they provide liquidity for it. Without them, there would be not enough liquidity on the market, and it would be difficult to buy or sell stocks, especially in bigger quantities, at any time.

Traders expecting rising prices are the *bulls* (the majority), and those who expect falling prices are the *bears*. A market where prices are rising for a longer period is a *bull market*. A market with falling prices is a *bear market*.

At any given moment, stock prices depend on supply and demand. In other words, the price movement depends on one thing: is it more urgent for the buyers to buy, or the sellers to sell? If the buyers feel more urgent, the price rises, if the sellers do, the price falls.

For everyone willing to buy or sell there are two possibilities: either to place a bid or offer and wait until someone hits it, or hit a bid or offer him/herself. Suppose the price is 100. If the buyers place their bids below 100 (at 99.50, 99.70 or even at 99.99) and the sellers place their offer over 100 (100.70, 100.50 or even 100.01), there is no business. Someone has to be ready to buy higher or sell lower. If the buyers start hitting the offers first, the price rises over 100. If the sellers start the action, the price moves down, under 100. The situation can change many times even in a few seconds, but if it is more often important for one side to take action, a trend will emerge.

In the long term the stock market is rising and provides a much higher yield than treasuries, bonds or other fixed income assets. However, this doesn't mean it is either constantly or gradually rising, and of course not all stocks go up, even over the long term. There are long falling and stagnating periods as well, and there are companies that go bankrupt, so it isn't as easy as just buying a stock and sitting and waiting for it to go up in value. Even long-term investors have to decide both when to buy and sell, and which stocks to invest in.

Adventurous moneymaking

During and after the 2000-2002 bear market, people began to doubt that the stock market was a good place to invest, even long term. On the other hand, just before 2000 many investors and analysts believed that the stock market was growing faster and faster. Both opinions are wrong. Ever since capitalism created its 'temple', the Stock Exchange, there have always been and will continue to be ups and downs on the market. This is evident if we have a look at the long-term chart of the stock market; the S&P 500 is a useful tool for

FIGURE 2.

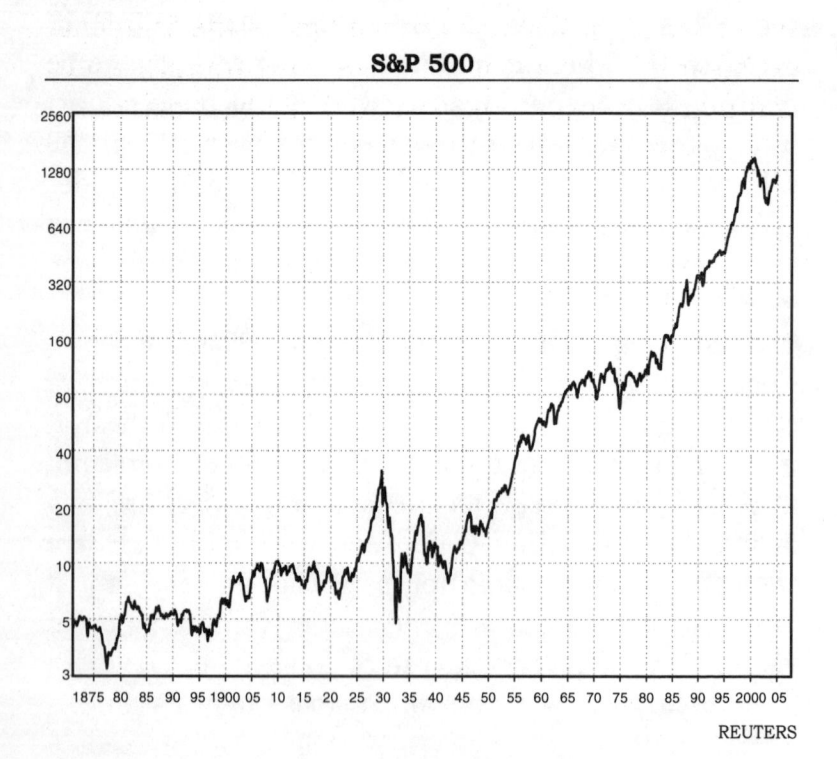

S&P 500

REUTERS

doing this because its 500 stocks give a broad view of the market as a whole. As we can see in Figure 2, in the long term it is consistently rising; the pullbacks are only temporary periods on the chart (although they can last years, sometimes more than a decade).

If we look at the last long-term market cycle since 1982, we see that it began at about 130 points, rising to 500 points by 1995, and then starting to rise much more steeply. That was the beginning of the bubble! It reached 1500 points at the top, and in three years' time it had dropped to about 800 points. If we compare this with its 130-point value twenty years earlier or even the 500 points in 1995 (the time of the 'irrational exuberance' speech), it is still a good overall result, and that was just the bottom after the bear market!

2. VALUATION OF STOCKS

Stocks don't have an exact value; if they did, there would be no need for the stock exchange as stocks would simply be traded at the exact value. Instead, the value of a stock is the price that one person is ready to buy at and another person is willing to sell at. Of course there are measurements that help us calculate the average value of a stock in the long term. However, these numbers show only the past and the present. Companies and their environment are changing all the time. Sometimes they make more profit, sometimes less, and sometimes they may even make a loss; there may be competitors emerging and so on. Similarly, the economy is constantly changing too, going through periods of boom and recession. Nothing is constant. The trader can only guess what may happen in the future.

Now let's examine some typical valuation numbers for a company's stock:

EPS (Earnings per share):
The EPS is the net profit of the company divided by the number of shares; for example, if a company's earnings were $600 million a year, and there were 1 billion

shares, the EPS would be $600 million/1 billion, or 60 cents a share.

Price-earnings ratio (P/E)
This is the most widespread measure used to value stocks, calculated by dividing the current price of the share by the EPS. For example, if the share mentioned above was at $12 on the market at the moment, then the P/E would be $12/$0.6, or 20. On the long term, the value of the P/E is about 15, but it is very difficult to use for individual shares. Profits, and therefore the EPS, are continuously changing, and of course there is no way to predict what the EPS will be in the future with any certainty; we have to rely on expectations and estimations. (There are a few people who know a bit more; these are insiders, and the behavior of a certain stock can show what they know.)

What is considered a 'normal' P/E ratio varies from stock to stock. For companies with a more or less constant profit, it is a bit lower (10-12), and for companies with shrinking profits much lower (in single digits). For an investor, the most important companies are those with growing profits (after all, that's why we buy stocks). For fast growing companies, the P/E can be well over 20. Imagine that our example company has a growth rate of 30%. It means that in a year's time the EPS will be 78 cents, rising to about $1 in two years' time. If the price remains the same, the P/E will only be 12 at that time. If it rises to $15, the P/E will be still 15 then, but the present P/E ratio is 25 ($15/$0.6)!

Those who are not willing to buy shares with a P/E of 20 or higher would have never bought Microsoft or other fast growing shares in the early 90s, and missed the giant gains. For growing companies and in strong bull markets, the P/E can of course be higher, but if it reaches 30, 40, or possibly even 100, as in the tech bubble in the late 90s, then the average investor should avoid the share. And once the earnings stop growing so quickly from quarter to quarter and year to year, we should avoid stocks with a P/E higher than 20 as well. For some sectors, the typical P/E is different; for example, for financials and utilities, it's usually lower, with a long-term average of about 10-12.

The P/E should only be taken into consideration when the EPS is at least 30 cents a share; if it is less, a small change in the earnings can mean a big change in the P/E value. And for shares of loss making companies, the P/E is meaningless, of course.

The P/E is also a very useful tool for looking at the average valuation of shares in a broader index. In this regard, the S&P 500 is the most significant. At the end of bear markets, it can drop to 5-7 (as it did in 1920, 1932 and 1982), while in bull markets it may go up to 20 or higher. In the stock market bubble that peaked in 2000, it was over 30, the highest in the history of the stock market.

BV (Book value per share):
The BV is the book value of the company divided by the number of shares.

Price to book value (P/BV)
The price to book value is equal to the price of the share divided by the book value per share. This is a useful measure, especially if the company has a small profit or even a loss, making the P/E useless. If the P/BV is one or less, the price represents a smaller sum than the book value of the company. If there are no serious problems with the company such as sharp losses or heavy debt, such a price is considered quite low. If the P/BV is 5 or higher, that is considered high, even for companies with big profits. Once the profit drops, the price can fall to a fraction of its former high if it's so far from the book value.

Market capitalization
The market capitalization of a company is the number of shares outstanding multiplied by the actual market price of the shares. There are small companies with a market cap of several hundred thousand dollars, but there are giants with a market cap of several hundred billion dollars. These are large-caps, the former are small-caps, and there are mid-caps in between. Large-caps are those with a market cap over $10 billion. Mid-caps are in the $1-10 billion range, and shares with a market cap under $1 billion are small-caps. The bigger market capitalization a share has, usually the more liquid it is. At the time of writing, the companies with the biggest market capitalization were General Electric and Exxon, both with a capitalization of about $380 billion.

3. OTHER FACTORS THAT INFLUENCE THE STOCK PRICES

Insider buying and selling

This is a very important indicator; insiders always know earlier and better what to do. If there's much more insider buying than selling, it is a bullish sign and vice versa. If a stock, especially that of a big company, goes against the market trend for a long period, then that may be insider action. Although there are more and more laws designed to combat insider trading, insiders such as the company management will always now sooner and better how their company is doing, and it is impossible to prevent them trading shares in their own company in possession of this knowledge.

Liquidity

A share is liquid if big quantities can be bought or sold with a relatively small price movement. The most liquid stocks are those having a volume of 30-50 million shares daily; not surprisingly, these are the biggest names: Microsoft, Intel, Cisco and General Electric, Vodafone in Britain, Deutsche Telekom in Germany, and Nokia in Helsinki. Those having a volume of about 10 million shares daily are very liquid as well. If the volume is between 2 and 10 million, the stock is still liquid, between 0.5 and 2 million moderately liquid, and under 0.5 million not liquid enough. Of course, a big fund needs much more liquidity if trading 100,000 shares a day or more; this requires a volume of at least 10 million. But for the regular trader, trading a few hundred or thousand shares, anything over 1 million is comfortable to trade. It is important to keep in mind that the bigger the daily volume, the smaller the volatility, and hence the risk, of a share.

Debt
If a company has heavy debt, it can be dangerous even if it makes a good profit. The interest paid on the debt and its installments can eat up profits, and once the profit drops, paying the debt can cause cash-flow problems as the company may run out of cash. If there's a debt and a huge loss at the same time, we should avoid the stock as it is likely to go bankrupt sooner or later, as happened to telecom equipment maker Marconi and Internet provider McLeodUSA.

New issues and corporate buyback
If companies decide to raise capital, they can sell new issues. If a lot of companies sell new shares at the same time, the quantity of the shares available (the supply) on the market increases, and this can lead to falling prices.

In other cases, when the market is depressed and companies consider the price of their own stock to be cheap, they can buy a certain quantity of their own stocks. This corporate buyback is usually a good sign because companies only do it if they have a rosy outlook and are expecting good earnings for the foreseeable future, and they know better and earlier than everyone else does whether this is the case! This is why corporate buybacks indicate a good buying opportunity for the mid- and long-term investor.

Dividends

Companies that make profits more or less continuously pay dividends to their shareholders; the dividend is their share from the profit of the company. Most companies pay only a part of their profit as a dividend, and others don't pay at all, keeping it for development or investment. In this case, it can raise the value of the company, and therefore also the share price.

Let's look at two examples. General Electric has been paying dividends every quarter for more than a hundred years. In contrast, Microsoft never paid dividends until 2003, using its profits for further investment, and thus the growth of the company, for 17 years. In 2003, as the pace of growth became slower and there was an enormous amount of cash in the company, it decided to pay dividends for the first time in its history.

Stock split

Share prices are usually between about 5 and 100 dollars/euros (in Britain, between 1 and 10 pounds). If the share is approaching $/€100, or exceeds it and stays over for a longer period, companies decide to split the share, which means that shareholders get more shares for their existing ones. Usually the market price falls in line with the ratio of the split, so the shareholders own about the same value after the split, but in some cases, the price falls less than the split ratio would justify, giving the shareholders an extraordinary profit. A typical example of a split took place with 3M shares, which were split at a ratio of 2:1. The price was $140 before the split and $70 afterwards.

Although most stocks are split when they exceed $100, there's one that has never been split: the stock of Warren Buffett's company, Berkshire Hathaway. The price of one share is $85,000, not an ideal instrument for small investors.

In cases when stocks fall to very low levels (under 1 euros/dollars or less), the company can declare a reverse split. In this case, the stockowners get one new share for 5 or 10 old ones. Usually the price of the stock jumps by the same ratio as the reverse split; for example, mobile phone maker Ericsson was at 80 cents in 2002 when a reverse split of 1:10 took place, after which the price was $8 a share.

Short interest
The short interest is the number of shares sold short at any given time. If this is a great portion of the outstanding shares (10% or more), the probability of a short squeeze, and thus a stormy surge in the price, increases.

Up-, and downgrades

As I mentioned earlier, the up-, and downgrades of analysts can increase the risks of trading. Even the most liquid shares like Intel or GE can make a sudden, big, unusual movement after an up-, or downgrade. Sometimes we can anticipate these movements, as the behavior of the share is often unusual before the grading due to heavy insider trading.

Sentiment

There are many comments about the market that anyone can read, mainly on financial web pages. The most important thing one can learn from them is the general sentiment, the opinions and expectations of the participants. If the sentiment is overwhelmingly bullish, a market slump is more probable. When the sentiment is bearish, it indicates that the market is oversold and there are a lot of short positions, so a rally is imminent. Of course, it's not always easy to judge the sentiment: there are often both bullish and bearish comments at the same time. In this case, the ratio of pessimistic to optimistic opinions can indicate the overall sentiment.

Scandals

Scandals, like Enron and Worldcom in America and Parmalat in Europe should not discourage traders. Things like that sometimes happen, especially after such a long lasting bull market, when it is easy to cheat investors and even banks and other financial institutions. But we should not forget that at the same time tens of thousand companies work well and successful. Maybe one advice: we should never invest our entire trading capital in one share!

Tips and rumors, information
Stock traders and even first-time investors like to give and take tips about stocks, market direction and so on. This can be one of the most dangerous things in trading because tips are almost always misleading. Those who originate and circulate these tips and rumors often have their own motives for trying to effect the market or a certain stock, so it's best to avoid trading on tips and rumors under all circumstances. Nowadays impartial information about stocks and markets is easily accessible on financial websites such as Yahoo Finance, CNN Money, Bloomberg, Reuters or the sites of online brokerage companies.

Factors influencing market trends in different time horizon
Long term, the most important factors are the fundamentals: the state of the economy, the state of a sector, and above all, the profit-making ability of a company, which is of course what we buy and keep stocks for, to make a profit. The investor gives money to the company; in exchange he expects a share of the profit.

The economy is more or less cyclical; there are booms and recessions. These are much 'softer' than 50 or 100 years ago due to increasingly sophisticated monetary and fiscal policy. The stock market has the same cycles, moving a bit earlier than the economy itself. The profit of most companies is in tight correlation with the state of the economy. In a recession, buying power declines, and so do sales and profits. If there's a boom, unemployment decreases, wages get higher, and the buying power of the consumers increases, so companies can sell more goods and services again.

Mid term, the most important factor is the level of interest rates. High rates and yields draw money from the stock market to bonds; investors are ready to buy stocks only at lower prices. When interest rates decline, investors aren't satisfied with the yields, so they tend to invest in stocks.

Low rates mean more money, and money feeds the stock market. High interest rates brought bear markets in the oil crisis in 1973-74 and 1981-82. After the crash in 1987, Greenspan lowered rates, helping the stock market immediately. From 2000 to 2002, the FED cut rates to historically low levels, but this time it took two years to have the desired effect on the stock market; the bubble was so big that it simply couldn't burst entirely any more quickly than this. The rally in 2003-2004 would not have been so huge without the incredibly low rates.

Short term, the most important factor is psychology. There are millions of traders on the market every day, influenced by fear, hope and greed; they often act under psychological pressure. If the owners of shares fear that prices could fall back, they rush to sell, causing the downward trend themselves. If the buyers with cash in their accounts fear that they might miss a beginning uptrend, they rush to buy aggressively, hitting the offers wherever they are, and in this way ignite the surge themselves.

So short and mid term, both money and psychology exert influence on prices. If both are positive, there's an uptrend; if both are negative, there's a downward trend, regardless of the state of the economy or the companies. If one is positive but the other is negative, there's a sideways market without a trend.

4. TRADING TECHNIQUES AND INSTRUMENTS

Market cycles: when to buy?

Now let's see what a trader can do? Kostolany says that both the rising and falling periods of the market have 3 phases. A good trader must act anti-cyclically; buying in the last phase of the falling period.

In this phase, most people are pessimistic. Stocks are just falling and falling every day, and no matter how deep prices are, some analysts set up new, even lower target prices. Of course there are also participants who believe that the market is oversold and therefore are expecting a rally, but they are outnumbered by the pessimistic point of view. However, an experienced investor knows that this is the clearest sign of the approaching bottom. At times like these it isn't easy to go against the crowd. The trader can feel lonely, and even if he is confident, he may change his mind at the last minute, swayed by the general pessimism around him.

Then, when everything seems the darkest, the market turns suddenly. Prices stop falling; there's no more stock to sell. In the first days, or maybe weeks, most participants don't trust the rally, seeing it instead as an excellent selling opportunity. This is the first phase of the rising period. In the next, second phase, as the market continues rising, optimists and pessimists are in more or less equal number. Those who missed the initial rally start thinking about jumping on the bandwagon.

The third phase is the overbought phase: when the public is more and more optimistic; everybody wants to participate in the 'bull market'. The same analysts who spoke about further collapse near the bottom now illustrate on their charts how prices are going to rise still further and set up new targets – this time high above the actual prices. It is not easy to imagine that prices can go any other way but up.

Then one day, suddenly a lot of sellers emerge. Many investors think it's only a correction and they start buying the dips. But prices cannot reach new highs again; on the contrary, they hit lower dips. This is the first phase of the bearish period. In the second phase of the fall, optimists and pessimists emerge in roughly equal numbers again, but prices just continue falling, with upside reactions. Finally the market enters the third, oversold phase and the cycle starts again.

The smart investor acts against the trend in the initial and final phases and with the trend only in the middle phase. In the oversold phase, he starts buying, going against the crowd. In the first phase of the rally, when the majority is still pessimistic, he keeps buying. In the second phase, he just sits on the stocks, and in the third, overbought phase he starts selling and just keeps selling when the market has already turned, in the first phase of the fall. In the second phase, he stays on the sideline sitting in cash (or in short position), and in the third phase, starts buying again. So two-thirds of the time he is going against the majority, going with it only one-third of the time. In order to do this, the experienced investor cannot let himself be influenced by the general optimism or pessimism that surrounds him.

This smart trader, as Kostolany says, need four things: money, ideas, patience and luck. He must have enough money to buy gradually in the last phase downside and the first upside, and to have the patience to wait if the trade is right but at first the circumstances are wrong. As we have seen, it often happens that two times two isn't four, but rather five minus one; it's the fundamental equation of the stock market, 2x2 = 5-1.

But what can the trader do if he hasn't got enough money? He has to follow another, more difficult strategy, the one Livermore followed. Livermore said the trader has to know the line of least resistance, and crucially, to recognize when it has changed. He cannot afford to buy downside during the oversold phase; he has to wait and identify the point where and when the line of least resistance has turned upward, and then start buying. Then, when the market is favorable, he can continue buying on a line up.

But how can we decide if the least resistance has turned and there is an upward trend? In an upward trend, the price moves higher after each correction, creating a continuously rising trend line. If it is broken and the stock cannot reach a new high, the upward trend is in danger and it is time to sell.

One thing is very important no matter which method one follows. Before any trade or investment, the investor has to weigh up the possible risk against the possible reward and face the question: is it worth trying? If the answer is yes, then he should go ahead, but if he's unsure then it's best to forget it. It's better to miss an opportunity than lose capital; as Livermore says, there's always another stock to buy.

When to sell: stop-loss and profit lock-in

If we open a position but it doesn't behave as we expected, we have to be strong enough to change our mind. We must draw a limit where we close the position, no matter what happens later: the most important thing is preserving our capital. Many traders and investors are not willing to take any losses at all, but this is the biggest mistake an investor can make. Take for example the case of someone investing in some high-flying tech shares in 2000. If he didn't sell with a loss, now those shares would be worth nothing. A good trader takes small losses and big gains. Everybody can be wrong, even the best traders, but if the loss is cut in time, it remains small compared to big profits.

Our biggest enemy on the stock market is often ourselves, and our fear, hope and greed. If we have a losing position, we hope that maybe tomorrow or the next day it will turn. If we turn a profit, we fear that the market will take it back. But we should be reacting in the opposite way, that is if we have a losing position, we should fear that the loss might increase, and if we have a winning one, we should hope that the profits will increase.

In other cases, the trader often becomes greedy when he or she has a huge profit. In this situation, people convince themselves that they can only win, so instead of selling the stock and securing the huge profit, they buy more to exploit the possible increase in price to the largest possible degree. But often this is the top, the end of the trend, and if so, the profit can quickly melt away.

If someone has a winning position, it isn't easy to walk the tightrope between cutting the profit too early and letting it melt down. The trader should ask every now and then: would I buy that stock now again? If the answer is yes, keep it. If no, get rid of it. It is also important to remember that if the stock we bought is rising but then falling back, we should never let it go in the red. Maybe it will just shake us off and rise further, but if not? A trader must be disciplined, a difficult skill to learn. He must be strong enough to cut the loss or not let profits melt away.

But what should we do if we have a big profit? In this case, we have more room to maneuver. We can let the profit grow, yes, we can hope, but only up to a certain point. We should decide in advance what fraction of our profit we are ready to let melt down, hoping that it's just a temporary setback; in my opinion between 30-50% is ideal. Less than 30% and we can be shaken off at every little correction, but more than 50% and we stand to lose more than half of the profit, which is too much.

For example, let's say we buy a share at $10 and have a profit lock-in of 40%. The price goes up to $13 and then drops to $12. Only a third of our virtual profit is gone, so we keep the share. Then it shoots up to $20 before falling back to $15. At $16 we sell it, because 40% of our $10 profit is gone. We have $6 in our pocket, and that's the point, no matter what happens to the stock later. Of course, it isn't easy to stay calm if it goes up to $20 again, or even higher. But we should never forget that it could go back down to $10, eating up our whole profit, or even lower, making a loss. It's impossible for a trader to buy at the bottom or sell at the top; what a trader has to do is make a profit.

Day trading

I have heard many people without much experience on the stock market say that they were planning to start day trading, thinking that there's a mathematical formula that can be exploited for this purpose. I always explain to them that if there were such a formula, all the smart traders would rush to exploit it and in the process make it useless.

In all honesty, I wouldn't recommend day trading. Nine out of ten day traders lose money and have to stop trading after a few months, when they run out of money. Day trading requires even more discipline than mid or long-term trading because there's only a few hours time to decide, and particularly when the position is a losing one, this can seem like no time at all. If one has so little money to invest that when he loses it he can replace it by working, then he can try day trading or any other kind of gambling. Those who have sufficient money to invest cannot afford this risk.

As Kostolany said, those who have a lot of money can speculate, but speculating is forbidden for those with only a little money, while those who have no money at all must speculate. (By 'a little money' he means a sum which is not sufficient for investing, but more than one can make and save by working, while 'no money' refers to a very little sum that can be made by working.)

Day trading is possible only on a volatile market with big price movements within the day. The more 'waves' there are in the price, the better. There were many days like this during the tech-bubble.

What if a day trading position goes the wrong way? One thing is sure: a day trade must be closed still during the day. The day trader must not get stuck in it under any circumstances; remember what happened with my Nvidia longs at $20.

Short selling

For most investors, investment means buying stocks. But prices often fall, often not unexpectedly, and we can make a profit out of these falling prices as well! There are three ways to do this: selling shares short, opening short futures and buying put options.

Selling short means that we borrow stocks (usually from the brokerage company or through them) and sell them. Sooner or later we must buy them back. We can sell shares short only on margin because no matter at what price we sell them, theoretically the price can go up infinitely so there's no limit to the possible loss. For example, say we sell a stock short at $20, and pay this price as a margin. If the price goes up to $30, we lose $10, but if it rises to $45, we lose $25, more than what we paid as margin!

In practice, it is enough to have a margin less than the selling price of the share, but we have to be careful if the stock is rising, because the broker can send us a margin call. My advice is to cut any losses immediately if the stock starts rising; a good trading position is going the right way from the beginning.

Futures trading

By trading futures we take obligation to buy or sell a share, a commodity or an index-contract for a defined time in the future (the expiry). If we buy (long position), we have to pay only a fraction of the price as a margin, and pay the full price at the expiry. In case of index-related futures and some other products that cannot be bought on the spot market, there is settlement at expiry without paying the full price.

If we sell (short position), we can sell a product we don't own, but we have to pay the margin as well. If we keep the position until expiry, in some cases (e.g. commodities or stocks) we have to deliver the products so buy them on the spot market if we don't own them. In other cases, such as index-related products that are not traded on the spot market, there's a settlement on the basis of the value of the underlying instrument, that is to say, the index.

As the futures price is in tight correlation to the price of the underlying product (the share, commodity, or the index itself), we have to pay additional cash as a margin if the price goes against us, but we can withdraw the extra money if the price goes our way. We don't have to wait until expiry to close the position; we can buy or sell our futures position at any time.

The trading of futures is a perfect opportunity for multiplying the risk and reward by trading on a small margin, and is also an excellent instrument if we want to make money out of falling prices. Although risky, if we follow some basic rules, futures trading can be a good option. First of all, the trader has to be more cautious and use stop-losses and profit lock-ins more rigorously than in the case of stock trading because with futures the danger is multiplied! If the margin requirement is 10% of the contract value, a 5% movement in the price makes a 50% profit or loss, and a 10% movement doubles our money or wipes us out.

One of the most popular futures contracts is the S&P 500, traded on the Chicago Mercantile Exchange. The trading unit is the index multiplied by $250, which means the price of one contract is about $250,000 if the value of the S&P 500 index is 1000 points, and a one-point movement in the index means $250 up or down in the price of the futures contract. As these are rather big sums, there is a smaller contract unit for individual investors, the E-mini S&P 500 futures. Its size is one-fifth of the big contract, so the value of one unit is about $50,000 when the S&P 500 is 1000 points, and a one-point movement in the index means a $50 dollar change in the futures price. As the S&P 500 rarely moves more than 20 points a day, the maximum daily risk or reward is about $1000 for each contract.

Options

An option means a right to buy (call option) or sell (put option) a certain stock, currency, commodity etc. The price of this right is the premium. This is appealing to inexperienced investors because they don't have to pay much to get started and there is the possibility of big profits when the underlying stock rises or falls. The risk seems limited; one cannot lose more than the premium, while the reward can be much higher. The problem is that the more volatile a stock is, i.e. the greater its probability of rising or falling, the more expensive the premium is. The trader's two enemies when buying options are high premiums and time pressure. For shorter expiry dates premiums are lower, but the chance of the anticipated price movement taking place within the shorter timeframe is also less.

I would suggest buying options in two cases, firstly when we expect a big, immediate move in the price of a share, and secondly when we expect an even bigger move but in the longer term. In the first case, we can buy options with an expiration date in the next one or two months, and in the second case with an expiration

Adventurous moneymaking

date in several months or one year. Of course, the premiums for these are more expensive.

The price of the option reflects the movement the market expects in the price of the underlying product. Those who sell the options (the short side of the option) expect a smaller price movement than the premium, and hope in this way to win the premium from the buyer (long side of the option). We should buy a call option if we expect a bigger rise than the premium and buy a put option if we expect a greater fall than the premium in the given time period.

For example, let's say a certain stock is trading at $45 and we expect a 10-point surge in the price within weeks. The price of the call option with a strike price of $45 with an expiry in two months is $3.50, so we buy it. We have to pay the premium of $3.50 per share immediately, and we have a right to buy the share anytime within the next 2 months at $45, or to sell the option at market price. If the stock falls, we lose the $3.50 but not more, no matter how low the stock falls. If it rises but only by a dollar or two, we are still in the red, but we lose only a part of the premium. If the price of the stock rises to $48.50, we break even, as the profit on the share covers the premium, and if the stock rises to $54 as we expected, we make a profit of $5.50 ($9 on the stock minus the premium).

Penny shares

Penny shares are those with a price of under $2. These stocks behave differently from those at higher prices because the minimal fluctuation is the same, one cent, no matter whether the actual price of a stock is $50, $5, or 50 cents, and whereas one cent is nothing in percentage terms for a $5 or $50 share, it is 2% for a 50-cent share. It only takes 50 ticks for the price to double or fall to zero.

In case of such a stock, steep rising or falling periods often last 3 or 4 days, during which time it can double or triple in price, or fall to a fraction of its price in percentage terms, all with only a few dozen (or less) ticks in the price. If there are buyers looking for a large amount of a penny share, let's say at a price of 50 cents, they won't want to buy 20 ticks higher because that is 40%, which they consider too much for one day. So they continue buying and the stock rises further the next day and at least one more day. By the time the buyers get the amount they want, the price has often doubled or tripled. The same happens if there are big sellers in such a stock, but of course downside.

A good example was Exodus, a telecom company, which fell from $10 at the height of the tech-bubble to just $1. A lot of buyers expected a correction, so they stepped in, but as they competed with each other, they pushed the price up about 40 cents a day, up to $3, or a 200% increase. Were it a $20 or $30 share, such demand would have pushed up the price not more than 5 or 6 dollars, or just 20-30%. A few days later, Exodus started falling with the same intensity, 30-40 cents a day. This time, it didn't even stop at $1; its final price before going bankrupt was 15 cents.

In Britain, where the penny or pence is the official name of what in Europe or the US are called cents, stock prices are denominated in pence instead of pounds and the rule is different: prices under two pounds are common and the minimal fluctuation is less than one penny.

Mutual funds
If an investor doesn't want to buy individual stocks, he can invest in mutual funds. These funds collect the investors' money and the fund managers decide which shares to buy for the fund. The biggest advantage of a fund is the possibility of diversification. A fund can buy hundreds or thousands of shares at low cost, while an individual investor can only buy a limited number of different stocks at one time.

In actively managed funds, analysts and fund managers are constantly trying to find the best stocks and invest in them. Most investors think this is the best solution and believe that fund managers can handle the portfolios much better than individual investors. In many cases this is true, but we have to bear in mind that funds often make a smaller profit than the market average (for example an index), or in a bear market, they can even make a loss. Over the long term, the S&P 500 beats the returns of 80% of actively managed funds!

When choosing a fund, we have to examine how it performed in the past. If it had a good profit from year to year (like the funds of investment guru George Soros in the 1990s), it has a better chance to perform well in the future. It is also wise to examine how it worked in bearish years. In a bull market, it is easy to achieve a double-digit return, but in sideways or bear market circumstances not many funds are able to do it.

Another thing the investor should take into consideration is the expenses of a fund. In most cases, they charge an annual fee. This can be anywhere between 0.1% and 3-4%. High fees can eat up a substantial part of the profit, and if the fund produces a loss, it even adds to the loss. Some funds charge extra fees when an investor purchases shares in the fund, or when he wants to sell them. These are unnecessary costs and by paying these, the investor can actually start his investment with a loss.

There are many kind of funds. An index fund follows the movements of a certain stock market index. The most common index fund tries to track the S&P 500 by purchasing all 500 stocks using the same percentages as the index. Others follow indices like the Dow Jones Industrial Average, the Nasdaq 100, Russell 2000 or any of the other existing indices. In a bear market, when indices are declining, of course there's nothing to do: index funds make a loss too. These funds usually have lower fees: as they are not actively managed, they don't need much staff. Buying the index constituent stocks in the right percentage is not a difficult task: even a computer can do it.

There are other kind of mutual funds: those investing into large-cap stocks, small-caps, shares of a certain industry or sector, or a certain country or region.

Adventurous moneymaking

When a sector or a certain market is becoming fashionable, investors start buying the funds investing in that specific market. For example, after a year of bull market in Eastern Europe, huge amounts of money were pouring into the Eastern Europe funds in 2004 and 2005. An experienced investor had bought these funds much earlier, when the bull market was just beginning. In the case of these funds, the timing is as important as in the case of individual stocks!

Hedge funds are similar to mutual finds, but they are less regulated and take much bigger risks (and of course in some case earn much higher returns). They open futures or short positions as well and buy risky shares that mutual funds usually avoid.

5. TECHNICAL ANALYSIS

Technical analysis involves analyzing the chart of a share, index, commodity, or currency, which shows graphically the price of the product over a period of time. This period of time may be a few ticks, ten minutes, an hour, a day, a year or even a century. On the chart, it is easy to see the price of a stock in the past. Technical analysis is a complex science and countless books have been written about it. Here I will just mention a few of the basics.

Linear or log scales

If a price of an instrument doesn't move too much on a chart, linear scaling is an adequate measurement. On a linear scaled chart, each vertical distance represents the same price change. But if the price change is too much in percentage points, it creates a distorted chart. If a price moves from $10 to $100, the first $10 increase, i.e. from $10 to $20, is shown as the same vertical distance as the increase from $90 to $100, but in reality, the first movement is a 100% increase, while the second is only 11% (see Figure 3, page 220). The solution to this problem is logarithmic, or log, scaling. In this case the same percentage of price movement is

Adventurous moneymaking

FIGURE 3, 4 *Line chart, linear and log scale*

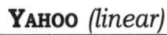

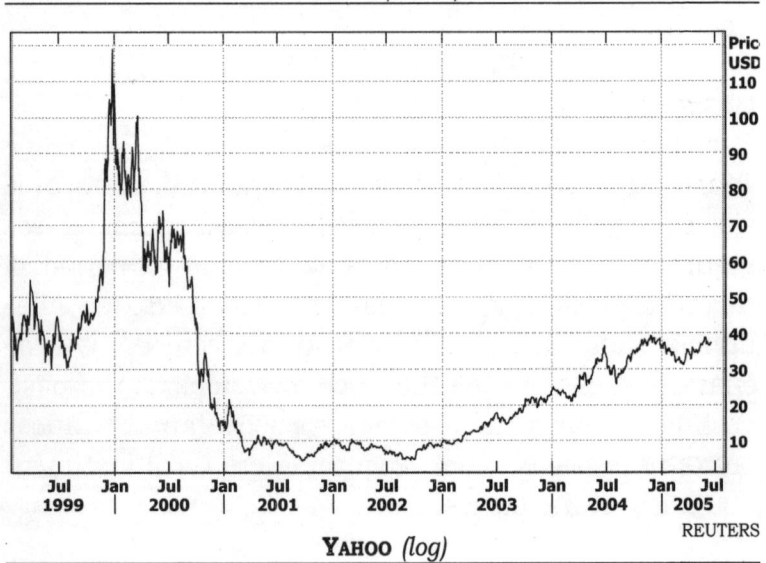

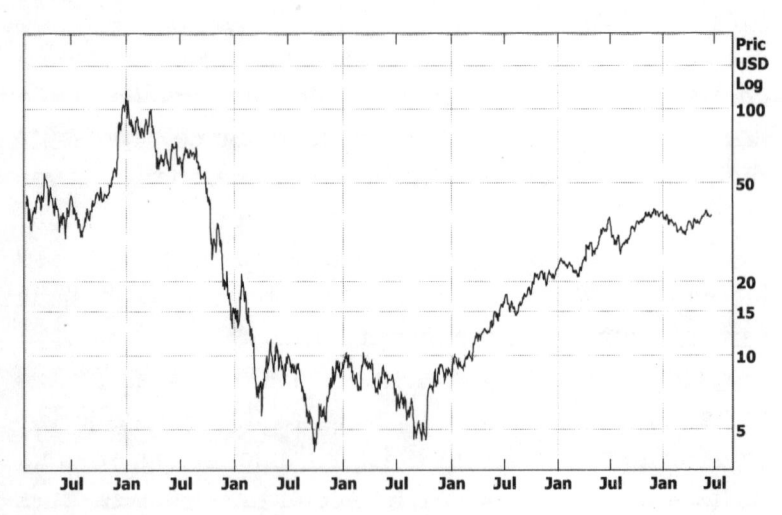

Technical analysis

shown as the same vertical distance on the chart instead of the same price movement, so the vertical distance is the same when the price doubles, no matter if from 5 to 10, 10 to 20 or 50 to 100 (see Figure 4).

Chart types

There are three different types of charts. On a line chart (see Figure 3, 4), prices, usually closing prices, are simply bound with a line. On a bar chart (see Figure 5), a given period, usually a trading day, but it can be a week, a month or just an hour or ten-minute period, is marked with a vertical line. The most common chart is the daily bar chart. The bottom of each

FIGURE 5 *Bar chart*

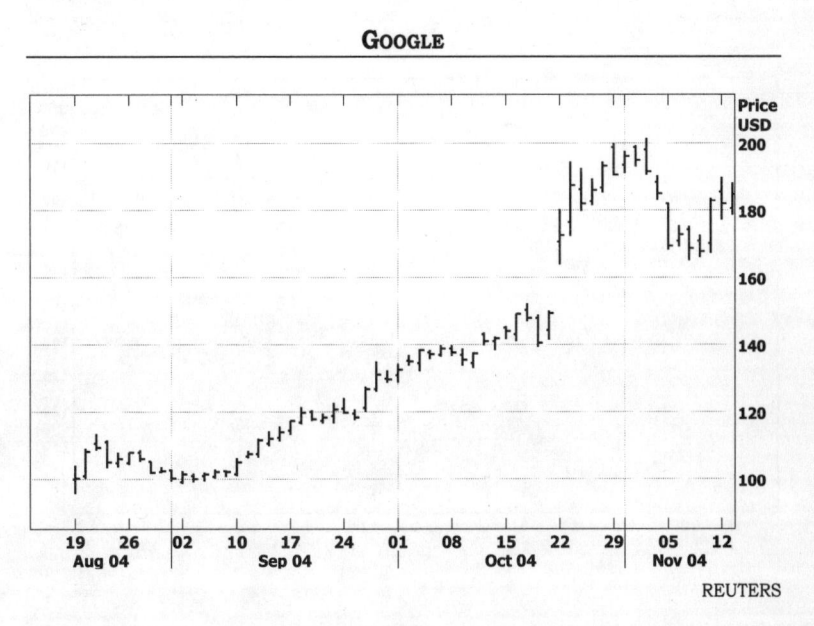

Adventurous moneymaking

vertical line is the daily low, the top is the daily high. The opening price is marked with a tick on the left side of this line, the closing on the right side of this line.

The candle chart (see Figure 6) is similar to the bar chart, but there is a rectangle between the opening and the closing price. If the rectangle is black (filled in), the closing price is lower than the opening. If the rectangle (the body of the candle) is white (empty); the closing price is higher than the opening. The vertical line over the body (the wick) marks the range between the daily high and the closing price, while the line under the body marks the range between the daily low and the opening price. Long white bodies represent bullish days (the

FIGURE 6 *Candle chart*

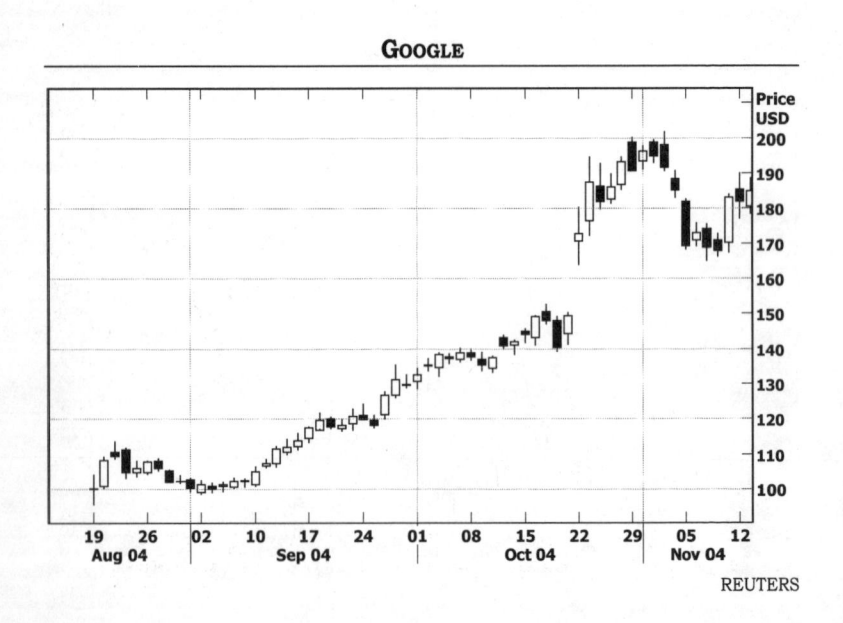

GOOGLE

REUTERS

Technical analysis

price rises a lot during the day and closes near the daily high) and long black bodies represent bearish days (the price moves a wide range and closes much lower).

Support and resistance

On the charts, we can see support and resistance levels as well as trends. A support is a level where the price stops falling and turns around. At that level selling pressure decreases because sellers consider the share too cheap or oversold and stop selling, while buyers become ready to take action. If the price repeatedly becomes the local support, it will form a horizontal support line. The resistance (see Figure 7) is the price

FIGURE 7 *Breakout*

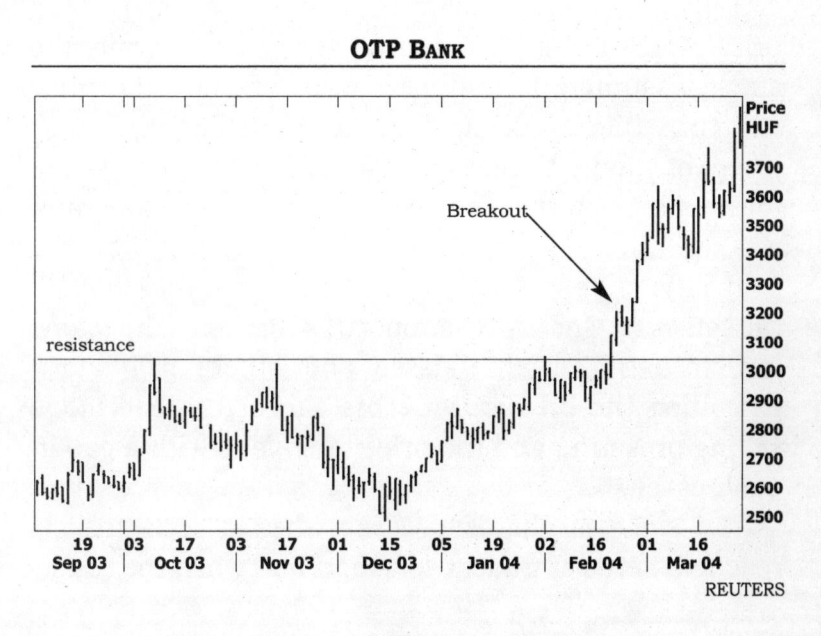

where buyers get exhausted and sellers become more aggressive. The more times the price tests a support or resistance level but doesn't break it, the stronger it is. If support and resistance lines are in an angle, they form trend lines.

If the price doesn't stop rising at a resistance level and goes over it, it is a breakout (see Figure 7, page 223), and the former resistance becomes a support. If the price falls back and goes below the line again, it is a false breakout.

If the price hurts a support and falls below, it is a breakdown. If it returns over it in a short time, the breakdown is false. If it stays under, the former support becomes a new resistance. The price often retests the broken level.

Millions of traders follow these levels. When a falling price approaches a support, they start buying the stock, assuming the support will work and the price will turn there and start rising. If the price doesn't jump, or jumps but less and less each time (i.e. sticks to the support), that means the support is weaker and weaker. There is a huge selling pressure but the traders who hope the support would not break buy all the stocks. Once the support is broken, the same investors trigger stop-losses and others sell short, exploiting the breakdown. This can create enormous selling pressure, and the price often falls with a gap in such cases.

The same mechanism works when a resistance is reached: herds of traders sell short and when the resistance is broken, they rush to cover immediately, often leaving a gap behind. Sometimes, after they have all bought their stocks, there are no more buyers and the price falls back below the level, forming a false breakout; other times, the upward trend continues and the price moves far away from the level which now acts as a support, as shown in Figure 7, page 223.

Overbought and oversold conditions

An instrument becomes overbought when it has risen too far too fast, and oversold when it has fallen too much in a short period of time. In such conditions, the Relative Strength Indicator (RSI) measures the extent of over-buying or over-selling on a scale of 1 to 100, with under 30 indicating an oversold market and over 70 an overbought market. An overbought or an oversold instrument needs a rest, either in the form of a correction or just a little pause in the fast rising or falling. This doesn't mean that an overbought instrument would immediately stop rising; first it may become even more overbought, but the more overbought it is, the bigger the probability of a correction is.

Reversal patterns

On the charts, there are countless formations; these are some of the most important:

A double top (M-shaped formation) occurs in a rising trend, when a price falls back from a high then rises again, but cannot exceed it the second time and falls back again. This indicates that the bulls are not strong enough to reach a new high and often marks the end of the rising trend.

A double bottom (W-shaped formation, see Figure 8) is the same formation but in a downward trend. The price cannot fall lower than the previous low; the

FIGURE 8 *Double bottom*

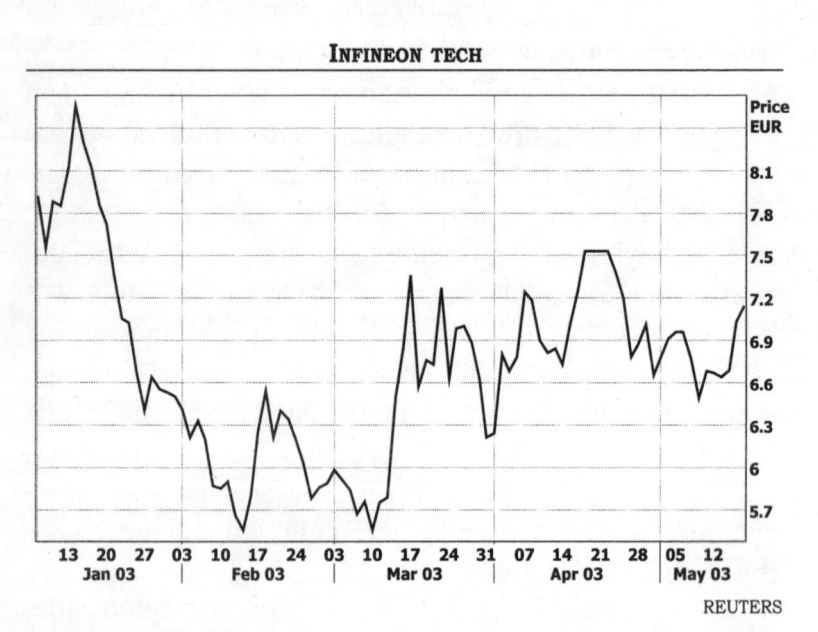

bears are exhausted. This often signifies the end of the downward trend.

The head and shoulders (see Figure 9) is a more serious indicator of a changing trend. In a rising trend, there are higher lows and higher highs. The left shoulder is part of this pattern. From it, the price falls back as a normal correction, then rises again to a higher

Technical analysis

high. Then it falls back to the previous low, forming the neckline. From there, the bulls try again but aren't strong enough to reach the previous high of the head, only reaching a lower one, the right shoulder. Then the

FIGURE 9 *Head and shoulders*

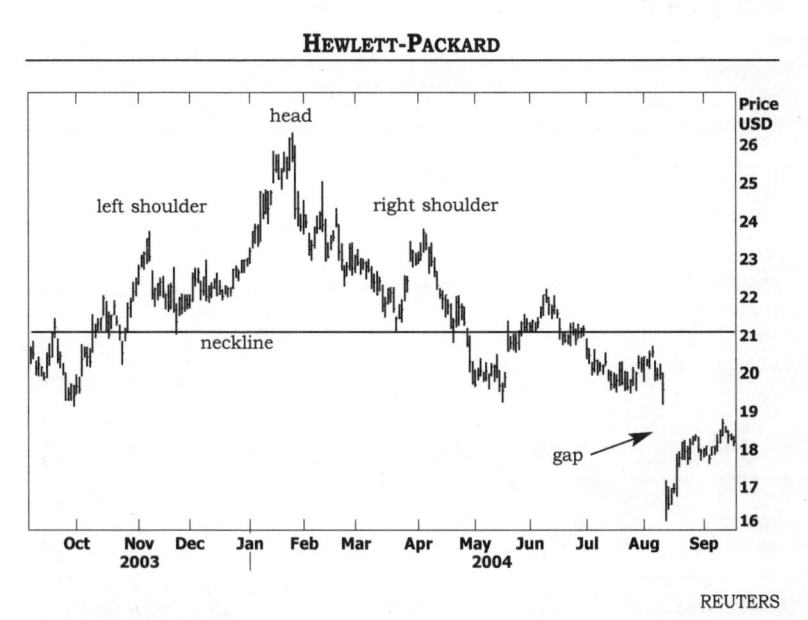

HEWLETT-PACKARD

REUTERS

price falls again, and if the neckline is broken, the reversal is complete.

PART FOUR:
Stock Markets, Indices, Shares

This chapter covers the most important markets and some emerging ones, their indexes and some shares. I have selected only a few dozen of the tens of thousands shares to discuss in detail, mainly those I have traded and have personal experience of. Some of these were chosen because they are popular among investors, others because they are good examples for different situations an investor may face (especially Nasdaq shares).

1. US MARKETS IN GENERAL

The biggest stock market is, of course, the American one, which became more important in the early 20th century, when the US became the most industrialized economy.

The US market is the most liquid market as well, attracting traders from all around the world who prefer American stocks because of their liquidity. German, British, and even Japanese investors trade in US markets, but American investors trade much less abroad. This way a bigger proportion of world capital flows to US equity markets than would otherwise be justified; this may explain why US stocks are still more highly valued than those in Europe and other markets.

There are in fact not one but several markets operating in the US. The New York Stock Exchange (NYSE) is one of the oldest and the most famous stock markets; on its Wall Street trading floor, trading is still going on the 'old-fashioned way'. The Nasdaq is a fully computerized market, like most other stock exchanges, making it easier to trade on it; this is why most companies that have gone listed on a market in the previous two-three decades have opted to be listed on the Nasdaq. The American Exchange is a much smaller market, but there are still some very important and useful instruments for the investors on it. In all there are 10,000 or more listed shares in the US, but of course only a few hundred are big and liquid.

A brief history of US markets

As early as the 19th century Wall Street was already characterized by periods of bull and bear markets. In the 1890s, when Livermore started trading, there was a big bull market with a top in 1901. Stocks became overvalued, but instead of falling they moved sideways for 14 years. During this time, companies' profits kept rising, so the stocks became fairly, or rather undervalued in historic terms.

During World War I, in 1915, another, although shorter-term, bull market started. For Livermore, it was an easy way to get out of debt and become rich again. The US didn't take part in the early years of the war, but US companies provided food, weapons and many other articles for the allied countries; the war fostered a strong demand for commodities, and these skyrocketed, too. As soon as the US entered the war, the bull market was over. From then until 1920, there was a bear market, with prices dropping to lower levels than 20 years previously.

The 1920s brought the big boom, which became a bubble and led to the crash of the stock market and the Great Depression of 1929-1932 (see Figure 1, page 81).

US Markets in general

It was very similar to what happened recently, when the bull market of the 1990s became a bubble that burst in 2000 and dragged the market down with it, just as had happened 70 years earlier. Fortunately, this time the effect on the economy was much smaller due to sophisticated monetary and fiscal policy.

The 1929-32 bear market was maybe the biggest in history; the S&P 500 tumbled 80% during this relatively short period (see Figure 2, page 190). From 1933 to 1937 there was a correction, but then came another smaller crash in 1937. It took more than 25 years to reach the level of the 1929 highs again! By this time, the same stock prices were not as overvalued as they had been 25 years earlier because the profit of the companies was that much higher. Of course, during this 25-year period there were several smaller bull and bear markets.

From the early 50s to 1966 there was another huge bull market; it was the time of the economic 'miracle' in the free, capitalist world. From the late 60s prices got into a bear trend again, which accelerated during the first oil crisis of 1973-74. A fast correction upside again, and then after some sideways years, the end of the second oil crisis in 1982 marked the start of the biggest ever bull market, lasting 18 years. Even the 1987 crash couldn't stop the bull; it was just a short intermezzo brought on by the fact that prices had risen too sharply in too short a period of time in the first half of that year, prompting the crash, which was in fact just an incredibly fast correction. During this long bull market, it was easy to get rich even with a small investment. Those who invested $1000 in Microsoft or Intel for example would have had several hundred thousand dollars if they'd sold in the year 2000.

Indices and the manipulating of the Dow

There are three widely-watched indices and several others which can be interesting. The most important is the Standard & Poors 500, consisting of the 500 biggest US stocks. It is broad enough to show the overall state of the stock market perfectly.

The Dow Jones Industrial Average has a big reputation, and as a result too many traders consider it the most important index. It consists of only thirty shares, so it represents such a small fraction of the market that it can be easily manipulated, making a market for other shares. And even not all of them are shares of the biggest companies! There are 10-15 stocks on the Dow which have a volume of only 1-3 million shares a day, compared to many others well over 10 million.

The weight of a stock in the Dow is in direct ratio with its price. For example, 3M at a price of about $80 has about three times the weight of Microsoft at $26, but Microsoft has a market capitalization of nearly 300 billion, compared to only 60 billion of 3M. In a realisticly calculated index, Microsoft should have a weight five times that of 3M, making 3M 15 times overweighed to Microsoft in the Dow at the time of writing. Thus, with a relatively small sum, the price of 3M and other smaller capitalization Dow components can be moved, and in this way the value of the Dow can be easily changed.

For example, some funds will sell tens of millions shares in the biggest companies. They buy the small Dow components with big weights (nominally higher prices), a few 100,000 each, pushing the Dow up about 100 points. The public says, the Dow is rising, let's buy everything! The funds can now easily sell the biggest shares, millions of each without a price movement, or even at higher prices, manipulating the market for their own ends. And of course, it can be done the opposite way as well. The small Dow components can be pushed down easily, the public starts selling, and it's easy to buy a lot of shares.

In order to solve this problem, the Dow components should be weighed in a ratio of their market capitalization, or there should be more, say around 100, stocks in the Dow, including more Nasdaq shares. The Dow was originally a NYSE index and is much older than the Nasdaq. In 1998, two big names, Microsoft and Intel, were taken to the Dow to improve the situation.

The third important index is the Nasdaq Composite, consisting of about 5000 stock. The Nasdaq is 'tech laden', which is why there was a much higher movement in the Nasdaq Composite than either in the Dow or in the S&P 500 during the tech-led bubble. Another good and widely watched index is the Nasdaq 100, which consists of the 100 biggest names listed on Nasdaq.

There are special funds holding stocks in a ratio of their weights in an index. This way, the shares of these funds represent the underlying index. They are perfect instruments if a trader wants to avoid the individual risk of a share, but has an idea about the direction of the general market or a segment of it. Some of the most important are:

DIA (Diamonds Trust)
It represents the Dow Jones Industrial Average. One share's value is the Dow Jones divided by 100, so when the Dow is 10,000 points, one DIA share is $100.

SPY (S&P Depository Receipts)
It represents the S&P 500 Index. One share's actual price is the value of the S&P 500 divided by 10.

QQQQ (Nasdaq 100 Trust)
It represents the Nasdaq 100. One share's actual price is the value of the Nasdaq 100 divided by 40.

2. NEW YORK STOCK EXCHANGE

General Electric (GE)
The giant industrial corporation, which produces a wide range of electric appliances and other products, has been on the NYSE for more than 100 years. The long-term chart of the stock reflects the general condition of the whole stock market. From 1965 to 1982 it was more or less sideways at about $1, from then there was a bullish trend that accelerated in 1995 when the price was about $10. It peaked at $60 in late 2000.

When the general market makes a positive reversal during the day, GE usually starts climbing later, so it can be a good opportunity to catch the rally. It rarely has sudden moves or gaps, so a stop-loss can be used at any time to reduce the risks.

I traded it only once, in November 2002. Most stocks and the indices had hit bottom two weeks earlier, but GE was still shrinking because the market expected weak earnings. I figured if it had been falling before the earnings release, it would surely rise afterwards. It seemed like a good opportunity for the stock to join the rally, so the day before the earnings release, I bought several thousand shares. I was right: the next day, it was rising even in pre-market trading as the earnings were better than expected, and after the opening bell it rose further sharply.

J. P. Morgan Chase (JPM)
This financial company is one of the largest in the US, with branches in a lot of countries. In times of crisis, like the 1987 stock market crash, the 1990-91 Gulf war or the Russian crisis in 1998, it fell a lot suddenly, but recovered quickly. Generally, financials are more sensitive in crisis or panic market situations. If JPM drops several dollars in panic selling in just a few days (just as in July and October 2002), it is worth buying for a sharp relief rally. In times of bigger financial crisis (like that in Russia), it can be a good mid-term investment.

An interesting story: in 2002, bankruptcy rumors circulating among brokerage houses pushed JP Morgan down to $15. It is the best and professional way of talking a stock down, but of course it works only when the general market is bearish for a long period, as it was in September 2002. The stock became so oversold that once the trend had turned, it surged 80% in 3 months. I bought it when it fell to and below $20, but I had to trigger the stop-loss as it tumbled further; I had bought into the falling knives. Finally, it reached $40, becoming one of the best investments among big-caps.

McDonalds (MCD)
McDonalds is one of the most 'visible' companies among those listed on the stock market. We can see its restaurants in every big city and along the roads, all around

the world. The hamburger giant is now more international than American: more than half of its 30,000 restaurants are outside the US. Over the past several decades, the stock has been one of the best long-term investments. If someone had invested only one dollar in McDonalds in 1965, kept it and reinvested the dividend, he would now have about a million dollars!

From a peak of $50 in 2000, the stock fell to $30 in two years, and then went into free-fall. There were rumors about a possible loss, the first time in the history of the company. It tumbled to $12 in a few months, and became an unbelievable bargain; from the bottom it doubled in just four months and tripled in two years.

3M Co. (MMM)

For a long time, this conglomerate's stock was the number 1 target of short sellers. When most stocks were falling and the Dow was tumbling, 3M was fighting the trend and remained at about $120. Investors considered it expensive, mainly because any price over $100 seemed quite high. It stayed between $110 and $130 for a long time before breaking out in July 2003 and soaring to $140, squeezing out most of the shorts. Then it was split 2:1 and continued rising to $90, or $180 in the old price.

Before the split, 3M provided one of the best tool for manipulating the Dow. Its weight was the biggest, with its nominally higher price, but its capitalization (about 50-60 billion) is much smaller than that of Microsoft, General Electric or Exxon (300-400 billion).

The AES Corp (AES)
This is an example of what a good bargain can be bought if the share of a good company undeservedly falls to a fraction of its former price. In the case of AES, investors punished this profit-making, stable power company just because it was in the same sector as Enron. As it was falling, I bought several times at about 5-6 dollars and sold with a profit of one or two dollars each time. But the big opportunity arose in the last months of 2002, when the price fell to near $1 (at this price, a share of such a company is a must), and the trend was turning. In a year, it rose to $10, in another year, to $18. What a multiplication opportunity!

Advanced Micro Devices (AMD)
AMD, a semiconductor stock, is much more sluggish than the semis on the Nasdaq. I often traded it as a stock left behind. I bought it at $20 in April 2001, when the rally had been going for two weeks, but AMD still remained near the bottom. Unfortunately I jumped off a bit higher higher only to see it soar to $30 in a few more days. That summer, like most of the semis, AMD crashed. It hit the bottom at $8, several days after the 'Taliban rally' started. I bought it at $10 but jumped off again. I should have waited a few more days: it reached $15 soon. At the market bottom in 2002, it tumbled even to $3, a fraction of the previous low, but unfortunately I forgot about buying it again. It had jumped to $9 and later to $25, or 700% in 2 years altogether...

There were several large-cap shares like AMD that were dumped at any price, even close to zero, in 2002. Buying in such an unbelievable oversold situation and sitting tight can mean a profit of several hundred percent, like in this case.

Micron Technology (MU)
Micron (MU) is another semi on the NYSE that didn't fall for long in the 2001 bear market, while others collapsed. The price was up at $40 and stayed there still for months after everything else started falling. I sold short there, and in the end the price tumbled to $20 in weeks. In the early 2002 bull trap it rose once again to $40. I completely neglected the share, which was of course a mistake. It would have been a perfect short selling opportunity once again: it fell to $10 in a half a year's time.

Lucent technology (LU)
Lucent is one of the few tech stocks on the NYSE that became a Nasdaq-style bubble. I never traded it, but at the turn of the Millennia, it attracted my attention when there was a profit warning and Lucent crashed from its $100 peak to less than $60, one step ahead of the other techs. When in March 2000 the Nasdaq reached 5000 points, it couldn't rise to a new high. Then in two years' time, it lost 99% of its value, falling to under $1, a perfect example of why it is a serious mistake to be stuck in a position without a stop-loss. Even after the big rally it reached only $4.50, a nice

profit for those who bought at $1 but cold comfort for those who bought anywhere between 5 and 100 dollars.

Weight Watchers (WTW)
Weight Watchers International, the weight-loss service provider, came to the NYSE in 2001. As I was familiar with the company (some friends were customers), I bought it on the very first day, a bit under $30. I sold it not much later at $37, finding that enough profit on a new issue, but it was still early. In less than a year it had reached $50 during the biggest slump on the market.

3. NASDAQ

Bellwethers

Dell (DELL): A stable tech
Dell, formerly known as Dell Computer, is one of the most stable companies on the American market. The stock was so strong that on two occasions it helped to turn the general market trend. First in April 2001, when a good comment on Dell ignited a huge six-week rally on the oversold market. Though it was just a bear market rally, the prices of many stocks doubled during that time; so it was an excellent trading opportunity. The second was a similar occasion in 2002, when the better than expected earnings ignited a broad rally.

Microsoft (MSFT): Buying in the dips
Microsoft is one of the biggest market capitalization stocks, with a staggering volume of 50-60 million shares a day. It was one of the best possible investments from the start of the company on the stock market in 1986. At its peak of $60 in 2000, it was 600 times higher than its opening price 14 years earlier, proof that long-term investment in stocks can make an investor rich, if he finds the right company at the right time.

From the top it fell to a third of its value, $20, at the bottom in 2002 (while most techs fell to a tenth or even less of their top prices), and then it jumped immediately. As a healthy stock, it jumps first and fast, and in the downturn, it usually falls last. That's why in an oversold market, it is an excellent buy with only a small risk.

Intel (INTC): A riskier large-cap
Intel, the processor maker giant, was almost as big a success story as Microsoft in the last 14 years of the twentieth century. From 1986, it rose from 30 cents to $75, or by 250 times. But from its peak it fell more than MSFT, to a bottom of $13. Though it is as liquid as Microsoft, Intel is more difficult to trade; there were two huge gaps (from $60 to $45 in 2000 and from $27 to $20 in 2002), which show that it can be as risky as some small-cap stocks.

Cisco systems (CSCO): Company buyback
Cisco was the fastest and biggest opportunity for investors to get rich between 1990 and 2000. The router-maker company started at 8 cents – splits and dividends adjusted – and peaked at $100 in 2000. Imagine: $1200 dollars from a one-dollar investment in only ten years... But of course, in the end it was a bubble and the price came down below $10.

Cisco was one of the companies that announced huge buybacks in 2001-2002. It was a serious buy signal. If such a giant company buys its own shares in big quantities, it means they already see their market turning (e.g. they have big orders for their products). In the end, it surged to $30. Tripling the price in one year, it's quite an impressive performance for such a big-cap.

Quallcomm (QCOM): A miracle in 1999
Qualcomm, a big tech name in the Internet and wireless sector, showed an incredible surge in just one year: in 1999 it rose from $6 to $180, or thirty times. That was the peak, with a second, lower high at $150 in March 2000, when the Nasdaq reached 5000 points. Then it dropped to $50, which became a support level for a long time.

I still considered $50 a very high price compared to others techs that were just crashing. I was sure it would go down to $20-$30, so I sold short several times, but it just didn't want to fall. Finally at the end of 2001, I started to buy put options on Qualcomm, usually with an expiry for the next month, and then when it expired with small gains, I opened another one for the next expiry, enabling me to follow it down to $30, with little gains every month.

The share became once again one of the best performers in the 2003-2004 bull market. From a bottom of $23 it surged 300%, to $90 (meanwhile it was split 2:1).

Internet stocks

Yahoo (YHOO): Big trends
Yahoo, the household name in the Internet sector, is a good example for big trends. It was $1.50 at the end of

1996, and it skyrocketed to $200 within three years. Of course, it became a bubble. It burst, and in just a little over a year, it had tumbled to $15. Isn't it a fantastic movement? As it started to recover, I bought it at about $22. After such a fall, I expected a recovery to at least $30. It didn't come. Instead, it tumbled to new low at $8.

Until then, the company had produced only losses. But then, in October 2002, after Yahoo's first profit-making quarter, the price jumped from $9 to $15 and rose continuously afterwards. In May 2003, two years after I expected, it reached $30 and kept rising, heading towards $40 and $50.

In 2004 it was split 2:1. I didn't really understand why, the price at $50 was far from three digit territory. Maybe for psychological reasons: the nominally lower price can make the stock desirable for the investors. Or maybe the company was sure the price would rise further and they placed their confidence in reaching the 100-dollar barrier in advance...

E-Bay (EBAY): Exceeding its bubble high

E-Bay is one of the most successful Internet companies, going to all time high just 4 years after the bubble. Not many tech stocks were able to do this! The online auction house became so successful that it proved: not all share prices were unrealistic during the Internet mania. The best companies in the sector perform well, the bed ones disappeared. Just as happened after the birth of each sector, in the past 200 years.

In the oversold market conditions when fast rallies began (April and September 2001, October 2002), it was a good opportunity as E-Bay was among the first stocks to jump. In 2004, it exceeded its year 2000 high by 100%! But it proved to be overvalued again (with a P/E well over 50) and in early 2005, when it became obvious that the profit of the company can't grow so fast as earlier, the price fell to its half within a few months.

Google

The share of the search engine company came to the market in August 2004. Pessimism was overwhelming before the public offering, so what else could the price do but skyrocket on the market? Those who bought in the initial issue at $85 or in the first days on the market were rewarded with a 100% profit in a few months' time. And those patient enough to wait a little longer, could harvest a staggering 250-350% as the share reached $300 in May and $400 in November 2005!

Exodus Communications: Falling to zero

Exodus was an Internet-related company that doesn't exist any more; it went bankrupt and disappeared. In 2001, it was falling fast from $10. It turned at $1, and rose to $3 in a few days, then fell to $1 again, and jumped a second time to $2.50. The third time it was coming down, I bought at $1.05. It fell to $1, but this time it didn't turn there. When it broke through $1 I triggered the stop-loss – but it was 85 cents before I could get rid of it all. Although my loss was just 20 cents, in percentage terms it's quite huge.

A few days later the share was at 30 cents, and in just a few weeks' time it had disappeared completely, worthless. Any investors who didn't sell in time, lost all their money. Many investors say they won't sell with a loss; they'd rather wait until the price rises back to the breakeven point, sooner or later. But this isn't necessarily a good idea; the price may never reach their breakeven point, but it can fall down to zero if the company goes bankrupt.

Chinese Internet companies: SINA Corporation and Sohu.com (SINA, SOHU)
These companies are the biggest success story and of course the greatest trading opportunity of the 2003 rally. SINA was only $1 in 2001. By October 2002 it rose to $2 where the fast rally started: in just nine months, it skyrocketed to over $50! Sohu was similar, under $1 in April 2002, the rally accelerated at $2 in October, and the stock was over $40 the next summer.

These companies were relatively small (market cap between 1 and 2 billion dollars) even after the fifty-fold rally. Of course the price of such a share can surge without limits, if the speculators of the whole world find it. If hordes of buyers want to buy Microsoft or Intel, they can do it with a price movement of $1, but if the same amount of money is aiming a stock like SINA or Sohu, the result can be a ten-dollar surge or more.

Semiconductor stocks

Semiconductors are one of the most popular technology sector with high volatility. Its main index is the Philadelphia Semiconductor Index (SOXX). It had an extreme high top over 1200 points in 2000 and an unbelievable dip at 200 points in October 2002. It is easy to trade the index: there's a stock of an index fund which represents it, the SMH.

Applied Materials (AMAT): Representing the general trend
Applied Materials is a big-cap semiconducor stock, one of the most liquid, with a daily volume of around 30 million shares. More or less, it follows the movement of the whole Nasdaq; so if a trader wants to trade the general trend but with more volatility, Applied Materials is a perfect instrument.

From its peak over $50 in 2000 it dropped to $20, then in the April 2001 rally it jumped from $18 to $30, in the autumn rally from $14 to $27, a year later from $10 to $18, and in 2003 from $12 to $25, or 50-100% in each rally. And when the general market falls, AMAT is a good instrument for selling short as well because it doesn't shake the trader off.

Nvidia (NVDA): Falling knives
Nvidia, the graphic chipmaker, is a good example of how dangerous it can be to buy into the falling knives, and how dangerous it is not to use a stop-loss on the

Adventurous moneymaking

Nasdaq, where anything can happen, especially with mid-, and small-caps.

Nvidia reached the top much later than the rest of the market, at the turn of 2001-2002 at $70. From there, it tumbled to $16 in just six months, followed by a quick correction to $23, and then another slide. I bought at $20 and the share closed at $19 on that day. I shouldn't have bought it (the falling knives), but having done so, I should have triggered the stop-loss that same day. In the next days, it fell further and further. I day traded it every time with a profit, covering the loss of the stocks I was holding from $20. I sold the last thousand shares at $12.70, before 3 more

FIGURE 10

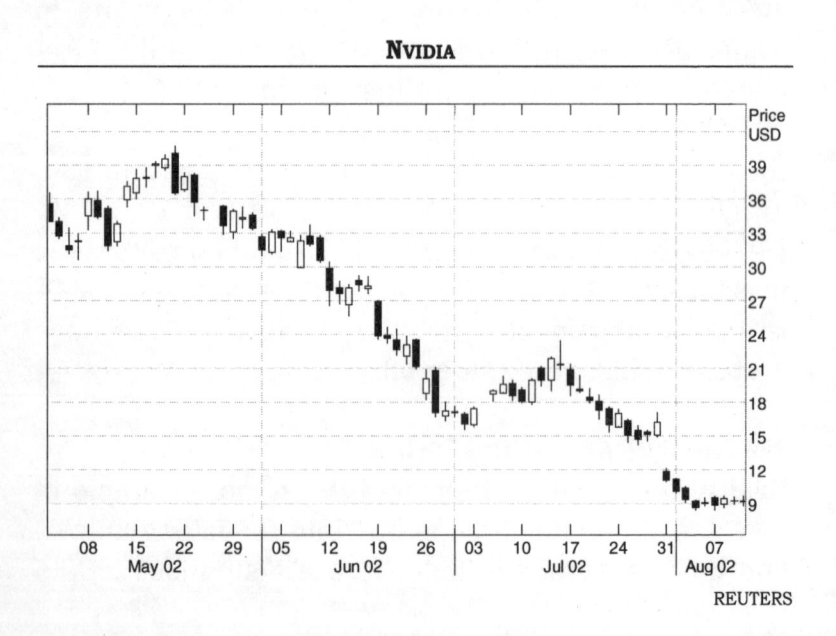

NVIDIA

days of tumbling, all the way down to $8 (see Figure 10).

Is it normal for a stock to fall from $23 to $8 in just 2 weeks? It may not seem so, but that's the reality of the markets. For mid-cap techs, the risks are big; not using a stop-loss and hoping instead can be fatal.

A year later the market justified my expectations: Nvidia surged to $27. And in 2004, history repeated itself: the stock fell below $10 in just 3 months. And then it surged to $30 again in another 7 months. Crazy a stock, isn't it?

QLogic (QLGC): Short squeeze

QLogic was a typical bubble stock: it was at $50 in October 1999, $200 in early March 2000, and $50 again in April. These are fast trends.

As it stayed at $50 while the Nasdaq was falling, I found it expensive and started to sell short at $50. Sometimes I made a dollar or two as it dropped a bit, but I never made much as the price kept jumping around just below or above $50 again and again. Maybe too many investors were thinking the same thing, that it was expensive so they'd sell short, and then when it didn't fall they closed the shorts, not letting the price down. In the end, when there were no shorts left, the price dropped to $20. It stayed there briefly in September 2001, but rose in the autumn rally to $50 again.

In the big sell-off in 2002, it tumbled once again, and in October it was back at $20. I bought it at $21, but it didn't rise that day, so I closed it out. In the next few days, it was a bit higher, and then, after a good earnings release, it jumped with a gap and was rising for weeks. I didn't dare buy it again, although I should have. The market was bullish and when this is the case, the investor has to buy if he thinks a stock is cheap, even if earlier he had sold it at a lower price.

It seems unbelievable but the stock reached $50 in 2003, for the third time in two years, and next year, it dropped again to nearly $20, just to recover again in early 2005. From $50 down to $20, then up to $50 again, not once but 3 times. That is volatility!

Broadcom (BRCM): Dangers of the after hours trading
Broadcom went on a wild ride during and after the bubble. In 2000, it was up at $250, and in 2002 down at $9! I traded it once after-hours and realized how dangerous the after-market can be, especially during the earnings season.

One evening, after better than expected earnings were released, I bought the share one dollar over the closing price, at $12. But an hour later, the company made negative comments on its outlook. The price immediately tumbled 2 dollars. The next day, it fell further so I triggered the stop-loss. In a few days' time, it turned once again as the whole market turned bullish, so I was shaken off. I should have bought it again, even at the higher price.

Traders often make this mistake: once they are shaken off by a stop but later proved to be right (2x2

= 5-1), they don't dare buy/sell the stock again. The trader should never look back! If he sold a stock at 100, but now considers it cheap at 200, he has to buy it at 200, no matter how much cheaper he had sold it in the previous trade. The circumstances may have changed, or maybe the market psychology has shifted. What seemed expensive yesterday may seem cheap today!

Others

Verisign (VRSN): A huge gap
Verisign is the other example, along with Nvidia, of how low a stock can tumble, regardless of how much it has already fallen. As it was tumbling from $30, I bought into the falling knives at $16. The next day there was a gap to $12 and the share closed at $10, and then the next day it tumbled down to $8 before rising up slowly to $11 and then going down again, this time below $5 (see Figure 11, next page).

This software stock was one of the biggest bubbles, and I heard about lots of people who got stuck with it. At its peak it was almost $300 and on the way down so many investors bought it. Even I, with my experience, suffered a huge loss with it. I triggered the stop-loss as early as I could but the loss was 25% – between one day's closing price and the next day's opening!

Two years later, Verisign surged to $35. As usual, 2x2 = 5-1: I had been right in the end, but along the way

FIGURE 11

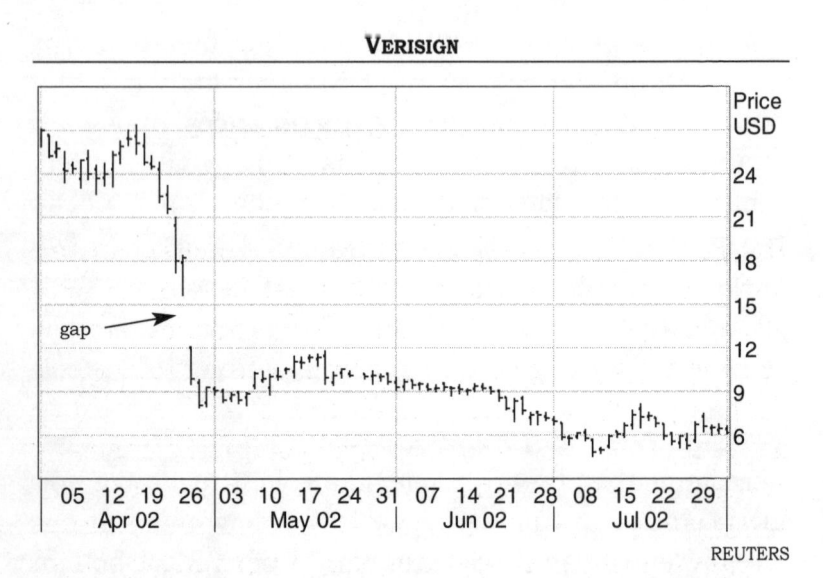

VERISIGN

[Price chart of Verisign from Apr 02 to Jul 02, showing a gap down in late April, with price axis in USD ranging from 6 to 24. Source: REUTERS]

things didn't quite go to plan. I found the right share but not at the right time...

Starbucks (SBUX): A new star

Starbucks is one of the non-tech stock on the Nasdaq. The chain of coffee shops is a very successful enterprise, in some respects similar to McDonalds. It's been growing continuously over the past few years, and the price of its stock has grown along with it. Looking at a chart of its growth, we don't see the same bull and bear markets as we do with tech stocks. Starbucks has so far been a good long-term investment and may continue to be for years to come.

4. LONDON STOCK EXCHANGE

The British stock market was the main market in the world for centuries. As the Industrial Revolution took place in Britain in the 18th and 19th centuries, Britain became the leading economic power. Without the Stock Exchange, the Industrial Revolution could never have happened; the textile, coal, shipping and rail companies needed capital, and this could only be collected at an efficient stock market.

The first stock market, the Royal Exchange opened as early as in the 16th century. The present London Stock Exchange is more than 200 years old, and until today, the most important stock market in Europe. Unfortunately, it has a worse risk to reward ratio than other markets because of a special charge, the stamp duty. Anyone buying a stock has to pay half a percent of its value as stamp duty, which in effect means that the investors have already made a loss as soon as they buy a stock.

The LSE and its index family, the Financial Times Stock Exchange (FTSE or Footsie), is much less volatile than other European markets, perhaps in part because there are fewer short-term traders because of the stamp duty; maybe this is the rationale behind it.

The most important index is the FTSE 100, containing the 100 biggest shares. In the early 90s it stood at 2000 points, and from there it soared more and more steeply until it reached 7000 points in the year 2000. After 3 years of bear market, the bottom, as elsewhere in Europe, was reached only in 2003, at 3200 points.

Vodafone

Vodafone is the most liquid share on LSE, with the biggest volume. In the peak of the bubble, the price of this mobile telephone provider was 400p. It was an excellent short selling instrument, as it fell from there more or less continuously to less than 100p. As with other telecom shares, the recovery wasn't too strong; Vodafone only rose back to 150p.

Meanwhile, it became not only one of the biggest British companies, but also a multinational enterprise, with branches in many countries. For years it produced a net loss but when it returns to profitability, the share could well be a good investment.

Marconi

Earlier I mentioned this telecom-equipment maker company that finally went bankrupt. The share price was as high as 1500p in the year 2000 (at prices be fore the reverse split), and was plummeting fast in 2001. Many traders (including my brokers and myself) bought into the falling knives, and lost a lot. But as I wrote earlier, not everyone had such a bad experience buying Marconi; my genius friend bought two million shares at 20p after it bottomed at 12p, and then the price jumped to 50p in just three days. From there, the stock fell again in 2002, this time virtually to zero; it was valued at less than one penny before the reverse split at a 1:5 ratio.

Baltimore Technologies
This was one of the most widely held shares during the tech bubble. I talked to many people who bought into it at every level, hoping that it would be a wonderful investment, but the company just kept making a loss and the price just kept eroding until finally it went bankrupt and the shareholders lost all of their money.

BT (British Telecommunications)
This telecom giant behaved in a similar way to its European brothers Deutsche Telekom, France Telecom and KPN. After reaching its peak at 1300p right at the turn of the Millennia, it fell relentlessly for three years, losing almost 90% of its value. The bottom was 140p; from there it rebounded to 200p in just three months.

ICI (Imperial Chemical Industries)
This increasingly multinational British group in the chemical sector was an excellent trading opportunity in 2003. At the beginning of the year it was trading over 200p. When the European markets crashed just before the Iraq war, ICI fell to 120p, and a bit later, after the market bottom, it tumbled again, just like Allianz and Munich Re in Germany, this time to 80p. After such a

sell-off it became an unbelievable bargain, a mid-term buying opportunity with low risk. In two months, it had risen to 150p, and in two years to 300p.

Reuters

The stock of this famous company was also a bargain in the European sell-off. Reuters has been providing and sending financial information since the birth of telegraph service in 1849. Before the Internet, it was the main, indeed almost the only, source of financial information and market data. When the Internet became widespread, the importance of the company decreased sharply, as all kinds of financial information and market data became cheaply available.

The company made a big loss in 2002. The price of the share collapsed like that of a tech share: in 2000 it was still over 1500p, but it tumbled to 200p in 2002, when markets reached the final bottom in the US. In March 2003, when European markets crashed, Reuters fell to 95p, an absolutely unjustified price.

Reuters adapted itself to the Internet era, becoming the main real-time market data provider and setting up a new trading platform, Instinet, which connects major markets around the clock and allows every institution to trade on it anonymously. The price of the battered share rose quickly to 350p (more than 350% in just six months), as it became obvious that the company was returning to profitability. When the 2003 earnings was released, it rose further with a gap and reached 450p within days, a rise of 500% in one year!

Marks & Spencer
The stock of this 120-year-old company moved almost independently of the market trend; the fundamental position of the company was the most important factor influencing its price. From a low of about 170p it rose continuously throughout 2001 and early 2002 and reached 400p, while the general market was heading down. Then it started falling, and while the general market was rising in 2003-2004, Marks & Spencer slipped back to 270p as the company lost market to its competitors, before a takeover bid pushed up the price 20% within one day!

5. DEUTSCHE BÖRSE (GERMAN MARKET)

The German market is quite volatile but not as risky as the Nasdaq. There are no giant gaps and endless movements without corrections, so a bad position can be closed with a relatively small loss. Its index, the DAX (Deutsche Aktien Index), was the most volatile of the main markets in recent years, reaching 7000 points during the bubble, falling to 2200 points at its bottom, and then surging over 5000 again in 2005.

At the bottom there was a 'Schlussverkauf' (final sale) the likes of which are very rarely seen. Shares of excellent companies, household names such as Allianz, Thyssen-Krupp BMW, Bayer AG, Siemens, and some German banks tumbled as if they would all go bankrupt. Investors rarely get the opportunity to buy such bargains.

Allianz
This big insurance company has been a good trading instrument in recent years. In 2001, a year after the market peak, it was as high as €400. From there it fell to €250 slowly, but in 2002 it collapsed to €70 in six months. There were many days when it moved up or down by as much as 10-15%. In early 2003 it tumbled

Deutsche Börse (German market)

further, to less than €50. And still after the market bottom, on the last day of March, it fell to €40, when Munich Re and Allianz dumped each other's shares. Then, over the next ten months, it tripled its price!

Munich Re

This reinsurer's chart is very similar to that of Allianz, reaching the top near €400, but its crash in 2002 was even faster, with very wild movements. It fell to €100 in a few months, at which price I bought into it, and from there it jumped to €150 in days. Around this time the share became quite volatile, moving €10 or more every two or three days, making it a good trading instrument. Every time it became extremely oversold, I bought it for sharp reactions and made a nice profit.

As it was tumbling again in early 2003, the upside reactions were hard to trade. The decline was relentless, and on the day of the 'cross-dumping' with Allianz, it fell to €50.

Deutsche Telekom (DT)

DT was one of the favorites during the tech boom. Its chart is a perfect inverted V-shape, as it rose from €40 to €100 and then returned to €40 between October 1999 and October 2000. The downward trend went on and DT became one of the weakest German stocks; in the slumps, it was among the leaders but in the bear-market rallies, it just couldn't rise. It reached bottom at €8, losing 90% of its peak value. After a correction, it dropped under €10 again on several occasions and I bought it then every time, considering it a bargain; it jumped each time, bringing a solid profit.

Infineon Tech
This semiconductor stock was the 'Liebling' (darling or favorite in German) during the tech-bubble, with a top of €100. I heard about German investors stuck in it while others were trying to buy it as a bargain on the way down, and I talked to one investor who bought it relatively cheap (€15), saw it rise to €30 and then let it fall down to €5.

If an investor has a nice profit on a share, it should never ever let melt down, or even worse, turn into a loss!

BMW (Bayerische Motor Werke)
This reputable carmaker is quite a good long-term investment. In the early 90s it was at €7 and from there it rose to its top of almost €50 in 2002, two years later than the market top. Meanwhile, in the 9/11 panic, it tumbled 40% in a few days, but then surged back 50% in another few days.

From its high of €50 it plummeted to €20 in early 2003, an unbelievable bargain for such a stable 'old-economy' company. From there it rose quickly to €40, or 100%! The share is worth buying every time a market rally appears to be in the offing.

Hypovereinsbank
This bank was possibly the biggest opportunity on the German market recently. It went to the sky still in the

Deutsche Börse (German market)

90s and reached its peak at €80 in 1998, long before the rest of the market. Over the next few years it fell by two-thirds, but the big crash started in mid 2002 when it fell as if it were worthless, to almost €5. But it was a share of a big, stable bank so it was obvious that there would be a huge rally, and the rally came. First it rose quickly to €10, then to €20, surging to four times its bottom price in just a little over half a year.

SAP

This German software-giant was maybe the best long-term investment in the 90s in Europe. It was selling at about €15 in 1995 and surged to €200 before the Russian crisis, then went even higher, nearing €300 in the bubble. Then it dropped back down to €100 and stayed long in the €100-170 range with wild movements, providing a good range-trading opportunity.

In 2002, like most other German stocks, it crashed. It fell to €70, and after a short correction down to almost €40 within days. At the brokerage company where I was trading, many investors bought into it at every level on the way down, and most of them were squeezed out; at the bottom, almost none of them had it.

Then the trend turned, and the stock rose even faster than it had fallen, 3-4 euros a day, and now the same investors started short selling. As these investors were squeezed, the surge became even faster and more furious. The price soon reached €80 and didn't fall back in early 2003, when most German stocks went to new lows. Later in the same year, it rose to well over €100, with much smaller fluctuations up and down.

DAXEX

DAXEX is the share of an index-tracker fund, just like DIA or SPY in America. Its value is the DAX divided by 100 in euros, so for example the value of DAXEX is €40 when the DAX is 4000 points. (In practice, it is a bit less, but that doesn't influence trading, as the difference seems to almost always stay the same.)

6. OTHER EUROPEAN SHARES IN AMSTERDAM, ZURICH, PARIS AND HELSINKI

ING

The Amsterdam Stock Exchange was the first stock market in the world. It was opened for trading the stock of the East India Company, still in the 16th Century. Today there are such famous names on the Amsterdam market as Aegon, Heineken, Philips, Royal Dutch, KPN, Unilever and the two banks; ABN Amro and ING.

Of these I mention in detail only ING. When there's a panic on the market this is as good a stock to buy as JP Morgan. In the Russian crisis it tumbled by 50% within weeks but as soon as the panic was over, it surged to almost where it had been before the crisis. The stock behaved similarly during the 9/11 panic, but the biggest opportunity arose in 2003 when all the European shares, especially financials, were dumped. It fell to €8, an unbelievable bargain for such a big bank. It jumped to €15 immediately, and in another few months it climbed over €20.

Panics such as the Russian crisis or that of September 2001 are the best opportunities for making money on the stock market. In these periods financials suffer most, but once the panic is over they rise with the same speed so it's advisable to buy them in such market conditions.

Swissair
This famous airline went bankrupt in 2002. When the stock tumbled to 0.01 frank one morning, I bought it fast. A stock for one cent, or to be precise one rappen; it couldn't be any closer to zero, and when the price reaches such a depth for the first time, it almost immediately jumps back up, even if it soon falls to effective zero (bankruptcy). I sold it at 0.07 frank an hour later, and not much later Swissair disappeared; the new company that stepped into its place is Crossair, which then changed names to Swiss International Air Lines.

Alcatel
The French telecommunications equipment maker was one of the European tech stocks that made the biggest downside movement after the bubble burst. In 2000 it was €100, while two years later it had lost 98% of its value and was trading at just €2. Those who bought it on its way down and kept it lost most of their money. However, the company wasn't bankrupt, so this price was unjustified. It jumped quickly and became one of the best investments in the 2003 rally, reaching almost €12, an increase of more than 500% in just a year.

France Telecom
France Telecom made even bigger up and down movements than its German brother; while Deutsche Telekom

peaked at €100, it reached €180, and two years later, when DT fell to €8, France Telecom tumbled to €6, losing 96.5% of its value.

The stock showed its first signs of strength much earlier then the general market, so after the bottom it seemed like a good investment, as indeed it was, surging from €6 to €20 in just two months. And in early 2003, while most European shares hit new lows, it did not fall back at all.

Nokia

The Finnish mobile phone giant opened for business in the early 90s. In 1996, the share price was about €2 and from there it surged to €60 in four years, giving those who recognized the importance and possibilities of this new industry a nice profit. For a period, Nokia became the most successful manufacturer of mobile phones in the world, controlling about 30-40% of worldwide production. Its stock can be traded in Helsinki, on the German market and on the NYSE as well, and it is very liquid on each of these markets.

As I've already said a lot about Nokia, here I'll just mention one more thing; whereas Nokia had earlier been a very volatile stock, in the new bull market it became rather flat. One possible explanation for this is that after the fast growth, the company's profits can be calculated long in advance; more or less predictable from quarter to quarter and from year to year without surprises, notwithstanding the occasional warnings or rosy comments.

7. EMERGING EUROPE

MTelekom

MTelekom is the Hungarian telecom company. Back in 1996 clever investors bought it from local councils still before it was listed on the Stock Exchange; in a ridiculous scheme, the councils had received 10% of the shares in state-owned companies from the state before privatization. The councils sold these shares almost immediately, at depressed prices, and as a result many traders got rich buying from inexperienced councils while the state missed out on a good source of revenue. The councils sold MTelekom at about 200 forints a share.

When it started to be traded on the Stock Exchange, MTelekom instantly went up to 1300 forints. During the Russian crisis it fell to 30% (I had expected it to fall further and stayed short, a big mistake), but quickly recovered. In the final tech bubble, it surged to a high of 2650 forints in early March 2000. Then the bubble burst, and many inexperienced investors bought into it. Finally, it lost 80% of its value in one and a half years and only recovered slightly.

I knew many people who were sitting on the share, hoping that it would get back up to the price they had bought it at, but the stock didn't rise at all while others doubled or tripled in the emerging market rally. It would have been much wiser to sell the stock and buy a healthy one instead. The main shareholder is now Deutsche Telekom, who owns 60% of the company.

MOL
MOL is the former Hungarian state oil and gas monopoly, now a Central European multinational company. I liked this share and traded it from the first moment it came on the OTC market and later on the Stock Exchange. It was a real cash cow for me: I caught it on its way up from 600 to 1000, from 1200 to 1350, from 2000 to 5000 forints, and again from 7300 to 15.000.

From time to time, other oil companies like Austrian OMV, Polish PKN or Russian Gazprom have bought or planned to buy smaller or bigger packages of it.

Richter Pharmaceutical
This share was a great success story in the 1996-97 emerging market rally, soaring from 1800 to 25,000 forints (from $12 to $120) in just15 months! The main market for its products is Russia, so the price of the share collapsed during the Russian crisis, but Richter didn't stop delivering its products to Russia when it couldn't pay. This turned out to be a good decision; Russia soon emerged from the crisis, paid its debts to Richter and as a result, the company was able to keep its market share in Russia, unlike many others.

OTP Bank

This former state monopoly has been able to keep its good position in the banking industry and is now a leader in the credit and debit card business, as well as in the field of mortgages. Because these fields didn't exist during communism, by introducing them OTP has managed to increase its profit on a continual basis. The company made acquisitions in several countries in Central and Eastern Europe so it became a regional multinational bank.

The price of the share was as low as 82 forints in late 1995, but had surged to 8500 forints by 2005. Having risen hundred-fold in 9 years (or about fifty-sixty-fold in dollar terms), OTP is the most successful Hungarian share; it was even able to rise against the general market trend in the biggest slump in 2001 and 2002.

PKN Orlen

This is the Polish integrated oil company, incorporating refining as well as a big wholesale and retail market, with several hundred petrol stations in Germany as well. PKN is planning to become a regional oil concern by merging with other oil companies such as MOL across the region. The two shares behave very similarly on the market. Until 2003, both stayed in a relatively narrow range, then when oil companies and especially Central European ones became fashionable, both tripled in less than 2 years and still continued surging afterwards.

Blagoevgrad-BT

This Bulgarian tobacco company was hovering between 20 and 30 levas for 6 long years. After it finally broke out of that range in 2003, the stock surged to 120 levas in just a year!

In October 2004, rumors started circulating that at a planned auction Philip Morris or British Tobacco would buy a huge stake in the company at much higher than the current market price. My friends and I immediately bought a lot of shares at about 125-130 levas. At the auction, none of the prospective buyers placed a bid! The next day the stock was trading under 100 levas: a good example how foolish it is to trade on rumors or so-called insider information.

8. RUSSIAN SHARES

The Russian stock market provided investors with the greatest opportunity to get rich in our times. On 31 December 1991, the old Soviet system still existed, without any private property. Then on 1 January 1992, as the red flag with the hammer and sickle disappeared, the wildest possible capitalism took its place. Privatization happened under a kind of lawlessness and some people like Mikhail Khodorkovsky and Roman Abramovich became incredibly rich by acquiring formerly state-owned property.

The stock market had already begun to skyrocket in 1996, as was happening all across the former Eastern Bloc at this time. In 1997-98, capital was pouring into Russia, the land of endless possibilities. Then in 1998 the country became insolvent and the same capital fled. Stock prices fell to unjustified lows; the Moscow Times Index fell from more than 1000 points all the way down to 150 points. Those who bought then, in the big sell-off, could make a fortune. In a year and a half, it had risen thirteen times to 2000 points, and in five years fifty-fold, to 7500 points! It is difficult to imagine another situation where a market index could rise by a factor of fifty and the price of some individual stocks by one hundred-fold.

The biggest and most important companies are those in the oil and gas industry, as Russia's economy is based on these national resources.

Gazprom

Gazprom is the world's largest natural gas company with a market capitalization of about $100 billion in 2005; it is responsible for producing 94% of the aggregate natural gas production in Russia and accounts for 23% of the world's natural gas output. The Russian government holds a 40% stake and enjoys a majority on the board of directors. Foreign investors are legally limited to buying shares through American Depositary Receipts (ADRs), which cost more than local shares that trade for Russians only. Those who were brave enough to buy the ADRs when oil and gas stocks started surging in 2003 were rewarded with a profit of several hundred percent within 2 years.

Sibneft

This huge oil company, extracting and refining oil in Western Siberia, was the main source of Roman Abramovich's incredible wealth. In the early 90s, the Russian state started mass privatization. Every citizen was to be issued with a voucher worth about $50 that they could exchange for shares in the companies that employed them or in any other former state enterprise. Just like the compensation notes in Hungary and Bulgaria, most people sold them for cash offered by smart people like Abramovich and Boris Berezovsky.

Adventurous moneymaking

In 1995, a company connected to Berezovsky and Abramovich got a stake of 51% in Sibneft, for just a bit more than $100 million. The oligarchs now owned a controlling share in an oil company whose reserves of more than four billion barrels were equivalent to those of Texaco, Chevron and Mobil.

In 1999, Abramovich had bought out Berzovsky, and continued buying at a new series of auctions, in this way achieving a more than 90% stake in Sibneft. From 2001, the company began paying dividends unprecedented in Russian history: about $1 billion a year, most of which wandered to Abramovich, enabling him to buy English football club Chelsea.

The stock itself was an excellent investment during the Russian crisis, generating a thirty-fold profit in just 4 years for anyone who bought it.

YUKOS

Yukos is one of the biggest companies in Russia, producing 20 percent of Russian oil. During privatization starting in 1995, some private investors led by Mikhail Khodorkovsky became the main owners. They paid an incredibly low price for the shares, valuing the whole company at only $450 million: 2 years later, the market capitalization was $10 billion. During the crisis in 1998, the stock fell to 5 cents, but rose 300 times to $16 in the next five years!

In October 2003, when Khodorkovsky was arrested in Russia, the price of Yukos immediately tumbled 35%. Then the share once again rose to nearly the all-time high, but in 2004, the company was charged with tax evasion. To pay the alleged taxes, YUKOS was forced to sell its natural gas subsidiary. The price of the share collapsed and was only 60 cents in 2005. Even at that price, it was 12 times higher than in the crisis in 1998!

Those investors who had listened to Kostolany and bought shares during the Russian crisis made a profit of 100-200 times their original investment, even if sold when the share had already fallen to half its top value. Can anyone dream of a better investment?

ABBREVIATIONS

ADR	- American Depositary Receipt
AMD	- Advanced Micro Devices
BOVESPA	- Bolsa de Valores de Sao Paulo
CME	- Chicago Mercantile Exchange
DAX	- Deutsche Aktien Index
DJIA	- Dow Jones Industrial Average
ECB	- European Central Bank
FED	- Federal Reserve System
FTSE	- Financial Times Stock Exchange
GDP	- gross domestic product
IMF	- International Monetary Fund
IPO	- initial public offering
LSE	- London Stock Exchange
LTCM	- Long-Term Capital Management
NASDAQ	- National Association of Securities Dealers Automated Quotation System
NYSE	- New York Stock Exchange
RSI	- Relative Strength Indicator
SEAQ	- Stock Exchange Automated Quotation
SET	- Stock Exchange of Thailand
SMH	- Semiconductor Holders Trust
S&P	- Standard & Poor's

GLOSSARY

Arbitrage Buying a stock, commodity etc. on one market and simultaneously selling it on another market at a higher price. Thus, arbitrageurs take advantage of temporary price difference between different markets.

Benchmark Benchmarks generally refer to standards or averages against which the performance of a security or an index can be measured.

Blue chips Stocks of the best companies.

Bonds A bond is a debt instrument with which the investor loans money to the issuer that borrows the funds for a defined period of time at a specified interest rate.

Bull/bear market A market with predominantly rising/falling prices

Collateral Assets that are pledged as security for payment of debt. In margin trading, the securities in the account of the trader act as collateral.

Distribution Flow of stocks from a few big owners to many small holders.

Dividend Part of a company's profits paid to shareholders.

Earnings season A period of time; when companies release their earnings.

Face value (or par value) The nominal value of a security stated by the issuer.

Fait accompli Something that has happened, about which it is to late to argue

Fiscal policy Government policy regarding tax rates and government spending.

Fixed income asset An investment that provides a return in the form of fixed periodic payments.

Follow-through Steep rising day on the stock market with heavy volume, several trading days after a market bottom. It usually confirms a starting up-trend.

Globex An electronic trading platform used for derivative, futures and commodity contracts. It runs 24 hours a day.

Greenspan, Alan President of the Federal Reserve System (the central bank of the United States), 1987-2006.

Glossary

Irrational exuberance An infamous phrase uttered by Alan Greenspan in 1996 to describe the overvalued stock market at the time.

Liquidation The closing out of a position, mainly because of the lack of sufficient financial funds (margin) necessary to keep it open.

Margin Money or collateral deposited by both buyers and sellers of futures contracts and sellers of option contracts that serves as a performance guarantee.

Margin call A call from a brokerage firm to a customer to bring margin deposits up to a required minimum level.

Maturity The date when the issuer of a bond must pay back the borrowed sum to the bondholder.

Monetary policy The regulation of the money supply and interest rates by a central bank, in order to control economic growth and inflation and influence currency exchange rates.

Open interest Total number of futures contracts that remain open at a given moment.

Open outcry trading Method of public auction for making verbal bids and offers on the trading floor.

Paper profit Unrealized capital gain in an investment. It only becomes realized when the security is sold.

Preferred stock A class of ownership in a corporation with a stated dividend that must be paid before dividends to common stock holders. Preferred stocks do not usually have voting rights.

Secondary market A market where investors buy securities from other investors instead of an issuing company.

Security An investment instruments that represents part-ownership in a business enterprise (stock or share) or loan to the issuer (bond).

Takeover bid A corporate action where an acquiring company makes a bid for another company. If the target company is publicly traded, the acquiring company will make an offer for the outstanding shares.

Treasury bonds Bonds issued by the government of a country.

Uncharted territory A price range; where a stock (or other financial instrument) never traded earlier.

INDEX

Abatix 180
ABN Amro Bank 265
Abramovich, Roman 272-74
ADR 273, 277
Aegon 265
AES 240
Afghanistan 113, 133-34
Albena 75
Alcatel 266
Allianz 135-39, 257, 260-61
Amazon.com 142
AMD 98, 113, 130, 240-41, 277
American Exchange 231
Applied Mat. 249
arbitrage 30, 50, 279
Argentina 40, 79, 144
Athens 85
Austrian schilling 10, 18-20, 23-24, 28-29
Austro-Hungarian Monarchy 30, 159
Australia 156

Baltimore Technologies 89, 257
Bangkok 156
Bank of England 87

banknotes 18, 77, 86
Bayer AG 135, 260
benchmark 52, 66, 68, 135, 145, 147, 175, 279
Berezovsky, Boris 273-74
Berkshire Hathaway 199
Berlin Wall 22
Black Sea 75
Blagoevgrad BT 75-76, 271
Bloomberg 201
blue chip 68, 70, 80, 102, 117, 279
BMW 135, 260, 262
book building method 167
book value 194-95
Bovespa 65, 156, 277
Brazil 40, 77-79, 144
Brezhnev, Leonid 13
British Telecom (BT) 257
British Tobacco 271
Broadcom 84, 89-91, 141-42, 252
Buffett, Warren 199
Bulgarian Telecom 152
Bulgartabak Holding 75
bull run 42-43, 129-30
buy-program 80

Canada 71
Caribbean 60
Chelsea 274
Chevron 274
China 153
Chinoin 44
Ciena 90, 104, 110, 114, 182
Cisco 89, 106-7, 110, 124-25, 196, 244
Clinton, Bill 47-48
CME 212, 277
CNBC 178
CNN 85, 97, 107, 201
collateral 175, 279, 281
copper 154
corn 49, 51
corporate buyback 197-98, 244
Croatia 146
Croesus Fund 59, 61
crown
    Czechoslovakian 30-31, 38
    Danish 18, 22
    Swedish 18
crude oil 62, 69, 137, 144-46, 153-54
Cuba 21
currency reserves 47, 62-65, 78, 149, 154
Czechoslovakia 21, 31, 38
Czech Republic 38, 145

DAXEX 136-37, 140-41, 264
day trade 113, 121-23, 182-83, 210
day trader 188, 209-10
debt swap 91-92
Delhi 156

Dell 97, 243
denomination 18
Deutsche Bank 135
Deutsche Telekom 89, 196, 257, 261, 266, 269
devaluation 18, 20, 23, 48-51, 62, 79, 148
DFCT 179
DIA 155, 236, 264
distribution 60, 63, 280
dividend 170-72, 198, 239, 244, 274, 280, 282
dot-com 90, 103
Dutch guilder 18, 22

earnings season 98, 252, 280
East India Company 265
Eastern Bloc 13, 42, 52, 272
E-Bay 142, 246-47
ECB 87, 277
El Nino year 59-60
E-mini 213
Enron 200, 240
EPS 192-94
equities 13, 32, 102, 108
Ericsson 199
Euro-zone 155
European Union 144
Exodus Comm. 103, 215, 247
Exxon 154, 195, 239

FED 54, 67, 69, 86-87, 94, 140, 155, 202, 277
Financial Times 40
Finland 177
fiscal policy 79, 201, 233, 280

Index

fixed income assets 189, 280
flight to quality 117
Florida 60, 71
follow-through 100, 280
forced selling 132
Fotex 26-27, 90
France 55, 115
France Telecom 89, 257, 266-67
Frankfurt 74, 95, 98, 156
free-fall 66-67, 108, 239
French franc 18
funds
    actively managed 216
    emerging market 52, 66
    hedge 67, 149, 188, 218
    index 217, 236, 249, 264
    mutual 188, 216-218
    pension 131, 188

Gates, Bill 187
Gazprom 269, 273
GDP 97, 130, 277
General Electric 126, 154, 195-98, 237, 239
Germany 21-23, 196, 257, 270
German mark
    East (DDR-) 10, 21-30
    West (D-, or Deutsch-) 17-25, 49
Globex 54, 97, 280
Gold 154
Golden Sands 75
Google 142, 221-22, 247
Great Depression 81, 232

Greece 85, 145
Greenspan, Alan 52, 54, 91, 99, 178, 202, 280

Heineken 265
Hewlett and Packard 187, 227
Hong Kong 58, 79
Hypovereinsbank 135, 262

IBUSZ 25-26, 35, 162-63
ICI 257
IMF 79, 277
Indonesia 58, 79, 144
Infineon 89, 114-15, 119-20, 126, 139-40, 226, 262
ING Bank 265
insiders 49, 64, 102, 193, 196
institutional investors 57
Intel 98, 119-20, 140-41, 182, 196, 200, 234-35, 244
IPIX 180
IPO 27, 41, 187, 247, 277
Iraq 133-34, 137, 153, 257
irrational exuberance 52, 54, 80, 191, 281
Italian lira 18

Jamaica 60
Japanese yen 49, 154
JP Morgan 67, 71, 126-29, 238, 265
Juniper 90, 104, 110-11, 116, 141, 182-83

Khodorkovsky, Mikhail 272, 274

Korea
　North 21
　South 58, 79
KPN 178, 257
Krakow 21
Kuwait 27

Lake Balaton 21, 25, 28, 53
Latin America 144
least resistance 106, 132-33, 139, 183, 206
liquidation 57-59, 67, 182, 281
liquidity 27, 67, 69, 188, 196-97, 231
Lithuania 145
LTCM 67, 277
Lucent 84, 241

Malaysia 58, 79
Marconi 103, 111, 127, 181, 197, 256
margin call 57-58, 211, 281
margin requirement 50, 212
Marks & Spencer 259
maturity 15-16, 281
McDonalds 238-39, 254
McLeodUSA 113, 197
Mexico 20, 40, 47-48, 79, 144
Mexican peso 47
Mexikoplatz (in Vienna) 24-25, 29-30
Micron tech. 241
MMM(3M Co) 199, 234-35, 239
monetary policy 78, 201, 233, 281

Mongolia 21
Moscow 48, 63, 65
Moscow Times Index 272
Mtelekom 68-71, 268
Munich Re 127-28, 132, 135-40, 257, 261

Nasdaq Composite 68, 84, 89, 235
Neftochim 75
New Zealand 85
Nvidia 121-22, 130, 210, 249-51, 253

oil crisis 62, 155, 202, 233
Ollila, Jorma 96
OMV 269
open interest 53-54, 281
open outcry 26, 42-43, 51, 74, 281
OTP Bank 145-46, 223, 270

Pacific 85
panic selling 57, 65, 83, 238
paper profit 59, 282
Paris 74, 265
Parmalat 200
patterns
　breakdown 127, 224
　breakout 80, 145, 223-25
　double bottom 68, 125, 226
　double top 120, 225
　head and shoulders 226-27
　V-shaped turn 137
penny shares 104, 113, 179, 214-15

Index

pharmaceuticals 44, 53, 135
Philip Morris 271
Philips 265
Pick 41
PKN Orlen 269-270
PMC-Sierra 89, 114-17, 130, 141
Polish zloty 16, 20-21
portfolio 72, 80, 132, 216
Portugal 145
Prague 21-22
preferred stocks 171, 282
pre-market 113, 122, 237
profit warning 95-96, 102-02, 121, 241
Puerto Rico 71

Qualcomm 84, 100, 104, 116-17, 141, 183, 245
Qlogic 89, 128-129, 251
QQQQ (Nasdaq 100 Trust) 155, 168, 236
rally
  bear market 90, 94, 96, 139, 243
  Easter 97, 99, 104, 182
  oversold 100, 110
  relief 91, 238
  Santa Claus 73, 131
  suckers' 97, 106
  'Taliban' 113, 183, 240
  year-end 131
recession 192, 201-2
Reuters 73, 201, 258
reversal 125, 133, 225-27, 237
reverse split 199, 256-57

Richter Pharmaceutical 53, 63-66, 269
Romania 21-22, 145-46
Royal Dutch 265
Royal Exchange 255
RSI 225, 277
Russell 2000 217
Russian rouble 62, 65
RWE 56-57, 60

Saddam Hussein 27, 133-34, 137, 144
Sanofi 44
Sao Paulo 156, 277
SAP 89, 139-40, 263
scandals 200
SEAQ 64, 277
secondary market 14, 16, 282
securities 14, 34, 282
sell-program 80, 129
sentiment 119, 200
SET 145, 277
settlement 37, 211-12
short
  interest 199
  squeeze 119-20, 130, 199, 251
Sibneft 273-74
SINA Corp 179, 248
Singapore 20
Slovakia 30, 38, 146
SMH 155, 249, 277
Sofia 75-76, 152
Sohu.com 248
Sopron 18, 20, 28
Soros, George 216

Southeast Asia 40, 58, 63, 85,
Soviet Union (USSR) 13, 23, 31
SOXX 249
SPY 155, 236, 264
stamp duty 255
Starbucks 254
stock split 198-99
Swissair 266
Swiss franc 18

takeover bid 172, 259, 282
tax evasion 275
Texaco 274
Thailand 58-59, 79, 144
Thai baht 58
Thyssen-Krupp 260
time pressure 213
tips 201
Tokyo 156
treasury bonds 49, 150, 164, 174, 177, 282
triple witching 139
Turkey 40, 79
TVK 55-61

uncharted territory 135, 143, 147, 282
unemployment 29, 97, 130, 202
Unilever 265

upgrade 65, 103, 119, 200
utilities 194

Verisign 84, 89-91, 121-22, 127, 130, 183, 253-54
Veritas Software 119-20, 141
Vienna 18, 23-24, 27-31, 169
Vodafone 196, 256
volatility 39, 64, 120, 145, 197, 249, 252
Volkswagen 135

Wall Street Journal 40
Warsaw 21
Weight Watchers 242
wheat 49, 51
Worldcom 179, 200
World Trade Center 107

Xetra 74

Y2K 83, 86, 175
Yahoo 84, 91, 99, 138-42, 220, 245-46
Yugoslavia 31
Yukos 274

Zalakeramia 64, 71, 91